The Anatomy of Urban Genocide

By: Charles Carpenter

The Anatomy of Urban Genocide

By: Charles Carpenter

Self-Published with assistance from
MIDNIGHT EXPRESS BOOKS

The Anatomy of Urban Genocide

Copyright © 2019 by Charles Carpenter

Self-Published with assistance from
MIDNIGHT EXPRESS BOOKS
POBox 69
Berryville AR 72616
MEBooks1@yahoo.com

Supreme Court Justice Thurgood Marshall

When the prison gates slam behind an inmate, he does not close his human quality; his mind does not become closed to ideas; his intellect does not cease to feed on a free and open interchange to opinions; his yearning for self respect does not end; nor is his quest for self-realization concluded. If anything, the needs for identity and self-respect are more compelling in the dehumanizing prison environment.

Dedication

This book is dedicated to my beautiful wife Maria Carpenter. I want to thank you for all of your love and unwavering loyalty and commitment. I love you forever and beyond.

Contents

Preface

Although America proclaims to be "the land of the free" yet when we take stock of America's residents we discover that America's mantra is a blatant lie!

Below America's veneer of power and wealth and below the deception of justice and equality lie the ugly truths regarding those who have been systemically deprived of equal access. To adequate housing, education, and employment opportunities. Those who have been victimized by such oppressive and often institutionalized biases are largely comprised of Blacks and Latinos. These stigmatized classes of people have been strategically manipulated into a lower socio economic symbolic prison commonly referred to as the ghetto or urban area.

The intent of my exploration of urban disparity is to understand the root cause of the diseased thinking which manifests itself in the behavior of those who hide behind a velvet veil of dignity and humanity; those who create laws biased toward minorities, those who are diabolical and oppressive, and maneuver with specific and deliberate intent to keep minorities locked in a lower socio-economic prison called the ghetto.

I will attempt to unravel the complex and intricate causes of the subtle and often covert economic crippling of urban minorities. This urban powder keg often serves as a breeding ground for self hate, jealousy, frustration, and ultimately urban genocide.

Acknowledgement

I want to take this opportunity to pay homage to all those who participated in this project and provided me with critical insight into the psychology of gang culture. Without your willingness to be transparent, this book would lack practical substance needed to reach our troubled youth of today. Thank you all for your time and commitment.

Special thanks to the following: Devin Jones from 9-8 Main Street Crips, Black from 9-7 East Coast Crips, Edwin Smith from Harlem 30's Crips, Eric Frazier from Rollin 20's Crips – Long Beach, Matthew Louis Johnson a.k.a. Louie from Bounty Hunter Watts Bloods, Mr. Callier from West Side Piru-Compton, and Mr. Danual Hodges a.k.a. Sugar Bear from Be Bop WATTS Bloods – 93 Street.

The Problem

Erimas Asghedom. Born August 15, 1984 known professionally as Nipsey Hussle. Nipsey Hussle was an American rapper and song writer from Los Angles California. Nipsey was a member of the Rollin Sixties Crips based in South Los Angeles.

According to police sources, on March 31, 2019 Hussle was shot multiple times in the parking lot of his clothing store, "The Marathon" in South Los Angles. At about 3:25 P.M. Hussle was hit five times in the torso and once in the head, two others were wounded in the shooting. All three were transported to the hospital where Hussle was pronounced dead. He was 33 years old.

The incident was tragic and unfortunate. This begs the question, why did this happen to such a musically talented young man who rose through the ranks of poverty to become a self made iconic rap artist?

On April 2, 2019 Eric Holder a 29 year old member of the Rollin Sixties Crips was arrested and charged with the murder of Nipsey Hussle.

Sources say Hussle was at his clothing store unattended by body guards because one of his comrades was released from prison after serving 20 years. Sources close to Nipsey reported that Nipsey wanted to provide his associate with a wardrobe to facilitate his transition back into society.

Allegedly Nipsey and Eric exchanged words outside of his clothing store. Supposedly Nipsey told Eric who had recently been released from jail that he didn't want him around the area because it was rumored that his release from jail was secured as a result of "snitching" on someone.

Sources also state Nipsey was scheduled to have a meeting with the Los Angeles police chief and other community leaders to discuss ways to curb and prevent gang violence.

Eric Holder may have been jealous of Nipsey's accomplishments, and when Nipsey audibly accused Eric Holder of being a "snitch," I believe those words pierced Mr. Holder's fragile ego and triggered his impulses which led to him shooting and killing Nipsey Hussle.

This situation has played itself out countless times in urban areas, although circumstances and faces are different, the common thread remains the same - jealousy!

Nipsey's untimely death raises several questions. First, why would a multimillionaire concern with whether or not Eric Holder snitched on someone? You would think that a young man of his financial status would concern himself with low level urban politics. I do understand the obvious loyalty Nipsey had to his neighborhood, and the Rollin Sixties Crips. However, I do believe that once you reach a certain level of success one has to disconnect without actually disconnection if that makes sense. What I mean by that is, it's possible to be supportive of where you come from while at the same time not making yourself a casualty of urban issues that are outside of the scope of your control. I believe that even if the allegation that Eric Holder did snitch on someone, it was outside of the scope of Nipsey's control - the damage was done and it would only be detrimental to Nipsey if he attempted to affect change regarding that issue. Nipsey had too much to lose by getting involved with that issue and unfortunately that mistake cost Nipsey his life.

According to criminologists large urban areas have the highest violence rates - hands down; rural areas have the lowest crime rates per capita, with the exception of low population resort areas with large transient or seasonal populations, typically have higher crime rates than the norm, this phenomenon has been observed in the United States and abroad. There are also different crime rates in other regions of the United States. For example western and southern states have had consistently higher crime rates than the Midwest and northeast. Criminologists are convinced based on this pattern that regional cultural values influence crime rates; others believe that regional differences can be explained by economic deferential factors.

Race and Crime

Official crime data indicate that minority groups are involved in a disproportionate share of criminal activity. African Americans make up about 12 percent of the general population, yet they account for almost 38 percent of violent crime arrests and 29 percent of property crime arrests.

Suspects who are poor, minority, or male are more likely to be formally arrested than suspects who are white, affluent or female.

Evidence of racial bias in the arrest process can be found in the use of racial profiling to stop African Americans and search their cars without probable cause of reasonable suspicion. Police officers, some social commentators note, have created a new form of traffic offense called DWB, "driving while black."

National surveys of driving practices show that young black and Latino males are more likely to be stopped by police and suffer citations, searches, and arrests, as well as are the target of force even though they are no more likely to be in the possession of illegal contraband than white drivers.

Another explanation of racial differences in the crime rate rests in the legacy of racial discrimination based on personality and behavior. The fact that U.S. culture influences African American crime rates is underscored by the fact that black violence rates are much lower in other nations - both those that are predominantly black such as Nigeria.

Some criminologists view Black crime as a function of socialization in a society where the Black family was tom apart and Black culture destroyed in such a way that recovery has proven to be impossible. Early experiences beginning with slavery have left a wound that has been deepened by racism and lack of opportunity. Children of the slave society were thrust into a system of forced dependency and ambivalence and antagonism toward one's self and group.

In an important work, All God's Children; the Basket family and the American tradition of violence, crime reporter Fox Butterfield chronicles the history of the Baskets, a Black family through five generations. He focuses on Willie Basket who is charming, captivating and brilliant. He is also one of the worst criminals in the New York State penal system. By the time he was in his late teens, he had committed more than 200 armed robberies and 25 stabbings. Butterfield shows how early struggles in the south, with its violent slave culture, led directly to Willie Basket's rage and violence on the streets of New York City. Beginning in South Carolina in the 1700's the Southern slave society was a place where white notions of honor demanded immediate retaliation for the smallest slight. According to Butterfield, contemporary Black violence is a tradition inherited from white southern violence. The need for respect has turned into a cultural mandate that can provoke retaliation at the slightest hint of insult.

Economic and Social Disparity

Racial and ethnic differentials in crime rates may also be tied to economic and social disparity. Racial and ethnic minorities are often forced to live in high - crime areas where the risk of victimization is significant. People who witness violent crime are victimized may themselves encourage violence.

Racial and ethnic minorities face a greater degree of social isolation and economic deprivation than the white majority a condition that has been linked by empirical research to high violence rates. Not helping the situation is the fact that during tough economic times, Blacks and whites may find themselves competing for shrinking job opportunities. As economic competition between the races grows, interracial homicides do likewise; economic and political rivalries lead to greater levels of interracial violence.

Even during times of economic growth, lower class African Americans are left out of the economic mainstream, a fact that meets with a growing sense of frustration and failure. As a result of being shut out of educational and economic opportunities enjoyed by the rest of society, this population may be prone to the lure of illegitimate gain and criminality. African Americans living in lower class inner city areas may be disproportionately violent because they are exposed to more violence in their daily lives than other racial and economic groups. Many Black youths feel a deep sense of helplessness and disparity a condition that elevates the likelihood of being incarcerated into adulthood. This frustration also manifests itself in Black on Black violence which leads to urban genocide.

Genocide is defined as the systematic, planned annihilation of a racial, political or cultural group. Tribes and empires have warred over natural resources and theosophical disagreements since humans learned how to swing a stick, but the end of the dark ages heralded a phenomenon that, by degrees threatens to destroy the very foundation of human civilization, and indeed the survivability of all life on earth.

Genocide, as it has transpired over the past five centuries began with the fall of the Roman Empire and the concomitant advent of the so called Christian Crusades. It is as if the teratogenic tribes of Western Europe unanimously agreed to subjugate and enslave the rest of humanity. Like a ravenous cancer the marauding hordes of conquistadors spilled upon the shores of the lands of Native peoples under the guise of religion, and spread disease, debauchery, and desolation upon the human race. In the process a mind boggling degree of plant and animal life was utterly exterminated - along with tribes, notions and sub - races of humanity - to an extent that now threatens the entire biosphere of planet earth.

Major aspects of teratogenic world domination include isolating humans from natural order of creation and from one another. This process included prohibitions upon the practices of cultural Native traditions, languages and even physical contact with family members systematically, psychologically, and physically traumatized, dehumanized and indoctrinated with a preternatural slave mentality commonly known as, "Willie Lynch Syndrome." William Robert Lynch was a 17th century slave trader who developed a nefarious and very effective training program to inculcate a self - replicating psychological disorder which severely decimates the victims sense of self and their ability to reason; making them mentally and emotionally dependent and child - like toward the master, but viciously antagonistic and distrustful of other slaves; especially those of their own race.

Racism, as a tool of psychological control was developed as a response to the confounding alliances that blacks, whites and red people were forming onto strong, resistance communities against slavery. Chattel slavery became a major component in the process of weakening those inter-racial alliances. The process ultimately led to the black community being systematically herded into urban concentration camps called "ghettoes" or "projects."

A "new deal"- type contract was struck with the white community which offered them a modicum of wealth and respectability in a relatively respectable sub-urban community which serves as a buffer zone between the Black people and the red peoples. Asian immigrants who come into the equation by the late 19th century were herded into mining camps, railroad work camps, and later their own urban ghettoes where white... Uncle Tom guilds worked feverishly to keep them separated and in sociopolitical contention with the Black community. Many "Latino" communities were heavy with African blood - Dominicans, Cubans, Puerto Ricans, Panamanians, Brazilians, and Guatemalans but conservative whites and their liberal constituencies worked to co-opt the Mexican, East Indians and Pacific Islanders within the urban and later the suburban communities. American society - and Eurocentric / ethno phobic societies throughout the world is designed to restrict the racial and cross cultural integration of the citizenry.

The world is a circle, and we are all in it together. The insidious control of earth's natural resources and the exploitation and dehumanization of people for capital gains - and the megalomaniacal being intoxicated with power is having a domino effect on every aspect of earth's biosphere vital to the sustenance of life on earth. The teratogenical processes that brought about urban genocide will lead to global annihilation.

Colors of Hate

I associated myself with gang members at a very young age of nine to be exact. My attraction to gang life was the idea of being part of a group, a sense of belonging, and having an extended family - big brothers that I never had.

I looked up to the older guys from my area and I modeled their behavior and mannerisms. I began to dress like them and participate in criminal activity because I believed that I would be able to solidify my position within the group.

Now that I've matured in my thinking 1 know now that my choice to be involved with a gang was foolish and severely consequential.

At this point in my life I'm looking for answers as to why I participated in certain unsavory activities as I grew up. The question that I often ask myself is how I developed hatred for rival gang members while I was an active participant in the gang life-style. How did I get to a place where I hated other black men based on nothing more than a color or geographic location?

I aligned myself with a Crip gang located on the Westside of Pomona called Tray - Five - Seven. I really can't articulate how I developed the mind set of hate based on what basically amounts to trivial factors. My only attempt to explain my mind set is by saying that I simply followed the example of the older members - they hated all Bloods, therefore, I hated all Bloods, it's as simple as that. I can't say that I gave thought to my decision to hate someone that in most cases I didn't know. I can only say that on my quest to be accepted I emulated what was acceptable to the group. Looking back I never had any real basis to hate, to hate someone that looked like me.

From a personal standpoint I made a big contribution to the

prevailing plague called urban genocide. I was taught dysfunctional thinking, and sadly I never challenged my warped thinking patterns until relatively recently. I modeled the behavior of individuals who were just as clueless as I was as to the justification to hate a rival gang member based on a color or a different geographic location. Some will argue that its deeper than mere colors or different housing locations. Some offer convenient justification by saying "the Bloods killed my homeboy."

I understand the reasoning behind their ideology having been a gang member myself. However, as long as we as a human race lack empathy, compassion, mercy, and forgiveness, the cycle of hate will continue to thrive. Until we stop justifying or making excuses regarding why we should hate, we will always be deprived of enjoying the full essence of life.

When we cultivate compassion, humility and empathy, only then will we be able to value someone else's well being. It starts with valuing ourselves first and that self - love will extend to those we come in contact with, but everything has to hinge on love.

I believe young inner city youth need to have positive role models to teach them, and model to them what success is - legally. I looked up to guys who were high school drop outs, guys that were illiterate, guys who were habitual criminals, guys who sold drugs, and these were the guys I wanted to grow up to be like - complete failures. I was blinded by the money, cars, and women that many of them acquired through the illegal drug trade. So in my mind it didn't matter if the so-called big homie knew how to read or not, it didn't matter if he was a high school dropout I saw what I viewed at the time as tangible results of being a successful drug dealer - instant gratification. Of course I know better now, I know that his success was always short lived. There was always devastating consequences associated with taking short cuts in life, trying to achieve instant gratification. I now guess those achieved what appeared to be a measure of success were later robbed and killed due to jealousy. I know one guy who became so successful that millions of dollars touched his hands, but today he has nothing to show for it other than a mind filled with regret and a prison cell that he paid for based on his choice to sell drugs and commit murder. He has now been in prison since 1987, and it appears that he will not be getting out any time soon. My point is this, there are no short cuts to success - delayed gratification is the only way to go.

I'm curious to know if other former gang members or current gang members share a similar perspective regarding how the hate developed. I devised seven pertinent questions that are used in the following interviews:

Devin Jones - Dee Man 9-8 Main Street Crip

Question #1: What was your attraction to gang life?

Answer: "I was infatuated with gang life because of my Uncles, and the respect they got from the community and the material things that came with it."

Question #2: What age did you join a gang?

Answer: "About 12 years old."

Question #3: What gang are you from and who are your rivals?

Answer: Devil Lanes Bloods."

Question #4: What caused you to develop hate for your rivals?

Answer: "My rivals did something to one of my family members and my fellow members; I felt it warranted retaliation, that's what fueled my hate."

Question #5: How did you personally contribute to the perpetuation of urban genocide?

<u>Answer</u>: "My subconscious thinking about gangs and drug dealing, and the part I played was participating in selling drugs and bringing down my community. This ultimately leads to urban genocide."

Question #6: If you could go back in time what would you do differently?

<u>Answer</u>: "If I could go back in time I would have never been in a gang, I would have brought something positive to my community. I would have went to school and become a politician to help my community. I had selfish thinking because I wasn't thinking about my community, I was only thinking of myself."

Question #7: What do you think it will take to eliminate the self hate amongst black males?

<u>Answer</u>: "One thing its gonna take, we don't have to leave our communities but our minds have to, we have to change the way we think and how we think. We have to look at each other as brothers and friends not as enemies, and a lot of prayer and education."

Matthew Louis Johnson

I posed the following questions to a member of the Bounty Hunter Bloods located in Watts California.

Question: What was your attraction to gang life?

<u>Answer</u>: "It was fun living dangerously while young, and it seemed to draw a lot of attention from females, I loved that, and the guys I ran with, they were like brothers that I never had, and everyone respected us."

Question. What gang are you from and who are your rivals?

<u>Answer</u>: "I was born into a gang, when my mom had me, she was with a gang member who was a Blood, back in 1968. My mother's

boyfriend was from a gang called Outlaws, and he used to always keep me with him, even before I started school. His homeboys were considered my uncles they raised me. My mom ended up breaking up with her then boyfriend when I was about ten. We then moved to another Blood neighborhood - the Nickerson Gardens Projects in Watts California - it was there that I met new friends who was Bloods, and because I have four very nice looking sisters, all the older gang members took to me to try to get to them, so I ran with older gang members. Our rivals consist of Grape Street Crips and Crips in general."

Question : What caused you to develop hate for your rivals?

Answer: " I got jumped by them (Crips) really bad when I was 12 years old in Junior High School, right in front of my girlfriend - my pride was hurt."

Question: What do you think needs to be done to eliminate the self-hate amongst Black males?

Answer: "I would personally gain an early education and influence my homeboys to do the same and become a positive figure in the community. I think it would take a great leader a respected black leader against injustice. For instance, Jim Brown had about 50,000 gang members at his house and there was no animosity no disputes - we need a strong leader."

Black, 97 East Coast Crips

Question: What was your attraction to gang life?

Answer: "My attraction to gang life was back then we kept it real with one another - there wasn't homies killing homies behind a fist fight."

Question: What age did you join a gang?

Answer: "I started my understanding of what gang life was about around the age of seven I could say - my street was headquarters."

Question: What gang are you from and who are your rivals?

Answer: "I'm a non-active member from 97 Street Neighborhood East Coast Crips located in South Central Los Angles. We have so many rivals, but to name a few: Swan Bloods are our arch enemies. Secondary to them is 92, 93 Bebop Watts Bloods, and Hoovers."

Question: What caused you to develop hate for your rivals?

Answer: "What caused me to develop hate for my fellow brothers? I lived in headquarters! I've been seen with members of my neighborhood and automatically I was treated as if I were from my neighborhood before I was officially a member. I've been repeatedly shot with guns! Disrespected with my mother present."

Question: How did you personally contribute to the perpetuation of urban genocide?

Answer: "I contributed to urban genocide by my loyalty to the game that hasn't been loyal to me! I planned and hunted rival enemies like I was duck hunting! It may sound ridiculous but its so true. 1 feel bad and I wish I wasn't brain washed with false beliefs."

Question: Looking back at your choice to be a gang member, if you could go back in time what would you do differently?

Answer: "If I had a choice to be from East Coast Crip or just be a regular man, I would choose being a regular man any day! I would bring our youth together in a unique way like never before! Finally, I want to give back to the community."

Question: In your opinion what needs to be done to eliminate the self hate amongst Black males?

Answer: No answer given.

Edwin Smith - Black Ed. Harlem 30's

Question: What was your attraction to gang life?

Answer: "I was attracted to the way they dressed to the power and control they displayed, to the attention they received from women and men, to the cars they drove. Also, the prestige that was received."

Question: What age did you join a gang?

Answer: "I was at the age of 13 when I started hanging out with gang members."

Question: What gang were you from and who were your rivals?

Answer: "I was a Crip from Harlem Crips Rollin 30's. Our rivals were all Bloods."

Question: What caused you to develop hate for your rivals?

Answer: "I allowed the older guys from my environment to influence me to believe other young Black men from surrounding communities were my enemies."

Eric Frazier (Rollin 20's CRIPS)

I interviewed Eric Frazier who is an original member of Rollin 20's Crips located in Long Beach California and he offered the following perspective:

Question: What was your attraction to gang life?

Answer: "Cars and clothes - low riders, brims (hats), Stacey Adams (dress shoes often worn by gang members in the 70's and 80's), leather coats, and the power and control gang members had."

Question: What age did you join a gang?

Answer: "9 years old"

Question: What gang were you from and who were your rivals?

Answer: "They call me Little Frazier a.k.a. Reese Cup, I'm, from Rollin 20's in Long Beach, and rivals are everyone who's not where I'm from."

Question: What caused you to develop hate for your rivals?

Answer: "Prison racial politics. When I was in prison in the early 80's white officers use to set Black inmates up, Black inmates would be the first to get shot and killed on the yard over a fist fight, they (Correctional Officers) would lie on rule violation reports, and white and Mexican inmates were always treated favorably while Blacks were treated with distain. So I started to develop a hatred for those who tried to oppress Black's."

Question: How did you personally contribute to the perpetuation of urban genocide?

Answer: "I contributed by getting others to think like I thought. I was the focal point of my hood, and what I did everyone followed suit, I led people onto destructive behaviors and thought patterns. In the beginning it was about urban genocide - the destruction of my fellow Black brothers, then prison politics caused me to shift my focus to Hispanics and the attacking of the oppressive establishments."

Question: Looking back at your choice to be a gang member, if you could go back in time what would you do differently?

Answer: "I would've played sports (baseball) and continued my education."

Question: In your opinion what needs to be done to eliminate the self hate amongst Black males?

Answer: "We need to reverse the "Willie Lynch" thinking we need to realize everyone is against us. We are the poorest, and we spend our money with everyone but ourselves."

Mr. Callier (YG GANGSTA BOO) Westside Piru Compton.

Question: What was your attraction to gang life?

Answer: "What attracted me to gang life was the glamorization of violence, brotherhood, and code of street conduct. Low self-esteem and lack of love and support from my parents made me decide to welcome and start normalizing criminality and anti-social behavior.

Question: What age did you join a gang?

Answer: "1 grew up around nothing but thugs, drugs, Crips, and Bloods. My mother was from 76th Street East Coast Crips and my father was a feared member of the notorious Grape Street Watts Crips. Both are well known and respected throughout their neighborhoods - bringing us back to the question at hand. I was born in Compton California, at Martin Luther King Hospital on October 4th, 1976 at 4:00 am. I was raised in my neighborhood by my grandma, a.k.a. Big Momma since a baby.

Growing up, I was already known and I knew everyone in my area. I know this is gonna sound impractical and irresponsible, but I grew up making myself believe I had no other choice and I was destined to follow in the footsteps of my parents! I was rationalizing irrational thoughts.

Anyway, besides already being a bad kid and crash dummy seeking acceptance unbeknownst to me the older kids were prepping and sizing me up for initiation! To make a long story short, at the age of 12 we all met up at Enterprise Park, Females and males of all ages, drinking and smoking while the music blared in the back ground. One of road dawgs (a good close homie) walked up and passed me a bottle of Cisco (Alcoholic beverage,) he waited until I took a beg swig and grabbed the bottle. Before I knew it, two more homies flanked me. Within seconds I was getting rushed by 3 homies. I told myself, this is it! Knuckle up or buckle up! Needless to say, after what seemed like forever. Two homies were on their pockets (knocked down) while me and my road dawg embraced, laughed and licked our wounds - so to speak, while the other homies and homegirls welcomed me to my new family (Blood in. Blood out! It's official!)

Question: What gang were you from and who were your rivals?

Answer: "The name of my gang is Compton West Side Pirus (134th Street.) I was known as YG GANGSTA BOO. My rivals were Crips, but those we considered true enemies were the infamous C. C. Riders a.k.a. Compton Crips. The ones that probably knew us and hated us the most were the Carver Park Crips, Mona Park Crips, Front Hood Crips, Nutty Block Crips, Trag Nu Crips, and Lantana Crips.

Question: What caused you to develop hate for your rivals?

Answer: "What caused me to develop hate towards my rivals besides the premeditated perception imbedded upon joining were personal run-ins, and isolated incidents."

Question: How did you personally contribute to urban genocide?

Answer: "I contributed to urban genocide by inflicting unspeakable acts of evil upon society and perpetuation the cycle of death.

Question: Looking back what would you do differently?

Answer: "Looking back, if I had the chance to do things differently I would have started by building myself worth through prayer, guidance and positive role models.

Question: What do you think needs to be done to eliminate the self - hate amongst Black males?

<u>Answer:</u> "I think to eliminate the self hate embedded in the Black male psyche, it has to start within. If one doesn't know himself he'll never begin to understand another. Hate is a feeling driven by thought."

Upon the conclusion of my various interviews I was able to gain a variety of perspective and insight into what I believe is a mental psychosis rooted deeply in the black male psyche.

Although different reasons were offered as to how we developed self- hate, I don't believe anyone should hate a human being based on race or ethnic background under any circumstances, but the fact is, racism in America exists in overt and covert forms. Black on Black hatred in my view is an utter oxymoron. For people of the same ethnic origin who in most cases share the same social construct, who live in the same poverty stricken areas, who are deprived and oppressed by the same conditions, yet hate each other and will even kill each other for trivial reasons is completely absurd.

22

The Cocaine Epidemic

During the 80's crack cocaine ravaged the lives of not just residents of urban communities, cocaine - or crack addiction - affected people of all economic and sociopolitical backgrounds. Crack cocaine didn't discriminate based on race or ethnic background. Although large segments of Black and Latino populations fell victim to what many believe was a well thought out plan to self destruct Black and Latino communities by virtue of the white substance called crack cocaine no one was exempt from the powerful clutches of rock cocaine, doctors, lawyers, entertainers, police officers, correctional officers, even government officials were victims of addiction.

Freeway - Rickey Ross was a referred to as a street legend who played a key role in distributing crack cocaine to various areas of Los Angeles County during the 80's.

Freeway Rick admits that he started his drug selling venture as an illiterate 28 year old aspiring tennis star. Although he shamelessly admitted during an interview that he was unable to read during the formation of his drug empire, he proudly expressed to a news interviewer that during his stint as a drug dealer there were days that he would make upwards of 1 to 2 million dollars per day.

In March of 1995 Freeway Rick was arrested in San Diego by the Drug Enforcement Agency (DEA) for selling to an associate to the Contra organization and an undercover DEA officer.

Upon serving 20 years in Federal, Rick Ross emerges from confinement literate and zealous about making a positive and legal impact on the society left behind in order to pay for his poor choice's and contributing to urban genocide.

As a result of Ricky Ross' position for change he has willingly and voluntarily agreed to give several television interviews in which he outlined the C.I.A. CONTRA CONTROVERSY. He eloquently articulated how the U.S. Government needed to fight a war in Nicaragua against the Sandinistas. Russia allegedly gave the Sandinistas 100 million in order to finance the battle with Nicaragua. However, congress cut off all funding to the Contras, leaving them vulnerable. As a result of the Sandinistas having a clear financial advantage, Regan and Bush had a vested interest in the Contra dilemma, according to Ross he believed the Government theorized that if Russia took over Nicaragua they would be too close to America.

Ross went on to say that he believed it would be beneficial to America to sacrifice a sector of people (urban poor Blacks) in order to save the Country from imminent peril.

Rick Ross believes, according to his own admission that the C.I.A. had knowledge of Contra members - who were on the C.I.A. pay-roll that were selling drugs, yet they (C.I.A.) turned a blind eye to their illicit activities.

Ross admitted during one of his many interviews that he had a direct link to various Contra members who were tunneling and selling drugs in the U.S. one of the members in particular was Danilo Blanden.

The following timeline will outline Blandon's activities leading up to his subsequent arrest.

1951 - Blandon born in Nicaragua.

1979 - Blandon flees Nicaragua with family to the United States and moves to Los Angles.

1980, February - Applies for political asylum in the United States.

1980 and 1981 - Blandon attends meetings of Contra support group in Los Angles.

1982 - Blandon meets Meneses who asks Blandon to sell drugs with the profit going to the Contras.

1983 - Blandon starts selling cocaine to Ricky Ross 1985 - Blandon's asylum request is granted.

1986, July - Meneses approaches Costa Rica DEA and offers to cooperate

1986, July - Meneses confidential informant provides information to F.B.I. in Riverside about Blandon's drug trafficking organization.

1986, September - Los Angeles Sheriff's Department open an investigation against Blandon's organization based on informant information.

1986, October - Los Angeles Sheriff's Department, Federal Bureau of Investigation and Drug Enforcement Agency exchange information about Blandon's organization and conduct surveillance.

1986, October 27. - Los Angeles sheriff's Department executes search warrants on residences and businesses of Blandon and his associates, seizing records but negligible amounts of drugs.

As Blandon's timeline continues it culminates as his close associate's turn informants which ultimately lead to the arrest and conviction of Blandon who was a key player in the intricate drug selling plot to finance a communist regime in Central America. Nor Meneses who was also a member or associate of the Contra was also involved in the plan to sell drugs to financially facilitate the Contra. Meneses later turned informant and betrayed Blandon. In the end Blandon begins to cooperate with officials by providing information, as a result on December 20th, 1993 he receives a reduced sentence of 48 months and 5 years probation.

1994, September - A motion was filed asking the court to reduce Blanden's sentence to time served and Blandon is released after having served 28½ months in prison.

1994, March - Ricky Ross is arrested by D.E.A. in San Diego after selling drugs to Blandon and an undercover D.E.A. officer.

Those aforementioned players played a pivotal role in the layers of crime, and dysfunction that saturated urban areas ultimately leading to the end result of urban genocide.

When I was a kid I remember people in my community refer to smoking cocaine as a "rich man's high." It was thought of as such because it was not easily accessible to poor people because of the high price of cocaine.

Comedian Richard Pryor was privy to the so - called "rich man's high" as he publicly admitted to "free basing" prior to the evolution of what later became known as crack cocaine.

Prior to the crack epidemic cocaine use was only within reach of those who had the financial means to afford such an expensive drug and Richard Prior definitely had the financial resources to afford to not just use, but abuse cocaine.

Richard Prior was using free base cocaine long before the crack epidemic exploded. In fact, Richard Prior was free basing so much cocaine that on June 9, 1980 while in cocaine involved stupor Mr. Prior poured 190 proof rum on himself and lit himself on fire. He was rushed to the hospital where he was treated for his self inflicted burns.

What's the difference between free base and crack cocaine you may be wondering?

Freebase cocaine is cocaine that is virtually free of the drugs hydrochloride additive. Free base cocaine is the result of the conversion of powder cocaine to cocaine sulphate. This new state makes the drug nearly 100% pure. For this reason, the drug now has a low melting point and is no longer water soluble, thus enabling it to be smoked. Freebase comes from using ammonia to extract the base. Diethyl ether is extremely flammable and volatile. This is a significant reason it is so dangerous to produce free base cocaine, and why there are so many explosions in drug labs that do so. The ammonia does not mix with the solution water and ammonia evaporating instead. Although freebasing produced a more intense high, because of the other components which are flammable, freebasing was very dangerous.

Crack cocaine is another form of cocaine and the most lethal of all. Using baking soda and heat, the crack is extracted from the cocaine powder resulting in a chalky rocklike substance. This rock is broken into small pieces and sold and is the easiest form of cocaine to smoke. Crack cocaine addiction is no joke!

My exposure to rock cocaine was in 1983 or it may have been 1982 - my memory is a bit cloudy regarding the time, however I do know that a member of the gang I was affiliated with showed me a small white rock encased in a small zip-lock baggie, and he said, do you know what this is?" I responded with a confused, "No!' Shamu was an older member of 357 Crips. I was 13 in 1983; he was maybe 17 at the time. We were on a street in Pomona named Belinda. Belinda was the main street that members of Tray - Five Seven met up at - headquarters if you will.

Belinda was also known for being an area with high volumes of drug traffic. Prior to the cocaine epidemic I remember the guys in my neighborhood selling Sherm - dipping sticks as they called it. Sherm was a street name for P.C.P... On this particular night when Shamu showed me that rock he was on the block trying to sell his product I ended up going to Juvenile Detention camp June 3, and 1 returned to the neighborhood in January of 1984. My freedom was short lived. I was rearrested and sent to the California Youth Authority I served 10 months at Fred C. Nelles located in Whittier, California I was paroled on August 23, 1985. When I returned to the community I discovered that the initial onslaught of crack cocaine was beginning to take shape. During this time Hip Hop Culture was in its early stages, the music at that time was riveting and socially and politically specific to the epoch of that era. Now children of low income parents were able to afford the latest name brand shoes and clothing such as Reebok, Fila, Gucci and Louis Vatton. Guys that didn't have a car were now driving the trendy cars of that time period Nissan trucks, Suzuki Jeeps, El Camino's, Cadillac's, and other nice vehicles.

Large profits were made from selling crack at the expense of someone becoming shamelessly addicted. Dealers didn't care about the damage they were causing by selling the poison known as crack, they were only concerned with making a fast buck.

Cocaine when smoked causes an extremely intense high that hits the brain within five to ten seconds, and the euphoric high only lasts five to ten minutes. Once the high subsides the user is left feeling depressed and yearning for more cocaine, hence the cycle of addiction begins.

In order to stave off the overwhelming feelings of depression more cocaine is consumed in order to feel that intense pleasure cocaine produces due to the massive release of the brains pleasure chemicals dopamine's and endorphins.

Those who fell victim to cocaine's intense grip were caught up in a seemingly never ending quest to feed that insatiable quest to smoke crack. Once cocaine addiction begins the devastation of the drug consumes all priorities if life.

Although my mother made a valiant effort to ensure that I do right, I was determined to be a thug. Even my parole officer (Su Wolfe) took a special interest in me for the sake of helping me get on the right track. I just didn't listen nor obey. Little did I know I would pay a dear price throughout life for not listening to counsel.

Although my mom was the one in my comer the entire time 1 was locked up, I put her on the back burner when I came home and sought out the so - called homies, who never wrote, never came to visit - nothing! Sadly, I would look for these people. I was trying to be accepted by people who cared nothing about me.

Instead of doing the things that an average fifteen year old would do, i.e. go to school, get involved with sports, and do homework and chores around the house, to a juvenile delinquent that lifestyle was boring. I wanted to live dangerously; I wanted excitement and the criminal lifestyle, this is what I was actively seeking, freedom with no boundaries. I've since learned through past experience that my thinking regarding boundless freedom was completely flawed. Freedom without boundaries is dangerous; boundaries are in place for our protection. Can you imagine a world with no traffic laws, no speed limit, and you could drive in any direction at any time? That would be disastrous to say the least. My mom and other authority figures tried to give me a measure of freedom with boundaries throughout my life for my protection, but I disregarded the boundaries with disastrous consequences.

I would disregard my mother's counsel and basically do what I wanted to do, I would also ignore the condition of my parole by association with gang members and those who were participation in criminal activity.

My feet were quick to run to badness, I had no regard for consequences, I lived in the moment and I worried about consequences only when it was time to pay for my actions.

I would always hang out in areas where drugs were being sold, weed was being smoked, and violence was a normal occurrence.

The area in my neighborhood that fit that description was a street named Jacqueline. Jacqueline was an area that was littered with low income apartments, and where there are low income apartments there's low income residents. The residents were welfare recipients, blue collar workers and senior citizens on a fixed income. You can guess what color most of the residents were - yes Black, poor and Black.

This demographic, a prime candidate for the cocaine epidemic. They were poor, barely scrapping by, and consumed with an overwhelming sense of hopelessness. Cocaine served as a temporary means of escape from life's seemingly insurmountable challenges. Many fell into that trap only to discover after that high subsided their problems were compounded.

Jacqueline Street was saturated with drug activity and high crime issues. When people of other nationalities came to purchase drugs they would often get robbed and assaulted. Looking back that was extremely bad for business. The object of any business is to keep the customer happy. We were young and foolish at the time.

Jacqueline offered nonstop excitement, the drug selling and drug buying was a nonstop continuous operation. I was fascinated by the excitement and the constant cat and mouse game of evading police detection. Although during the day Jacqueline Street offered a small measure of excitement, people seemed to appear in throngs under the cover of darkness.

With the influx of cocaine into the urban areas came crack experimentation. During this time a lot of people were curious about the rush that cocaine produced that everyone formally referred to as a "rich man's high." Back then cocaine was sold at street level increments of twenty five and fifty dollars. Back then there was no such thing as five dollar or ten dollar hits. It was twenty five or fifty dollar rocks called quarters and five - O's.

Many people during this time were smoking what we called "primos" a primo is a marijuana joint laced with cocaine. I was addicted to the speedy sensation of the cocaine followed by the mellowing effect of the marijuana. This form of smoking cocaine was somewhat accepted in some circles. However, smoking any form of cocaine in the gang subculture was frowned upon, although I knew several gang members who became addicted to cocaine by virtue of smoking primos. The ultimate taboo for gang members was to become addicted to smoking cocaine through the pipe, as that was viewed in the Black community as the most shameful act one could engage in, in terms of using drugs. Unfortunately, I fell victim to the strong guerilla known as crack addiction. Here's how it all happened:

One early October night of 1985 me and several members of Tray-five-seven were in one of Jacqueline Street's alley's waiting for cars to drive through so we could sell rocks to them. On any given night there were at least five people in the alley competing for crack sales. In those days a car would drive up roll their window down and express their desire to purchase cocaine and immediately at least three guys would motion to the driver's side - or passenger side and stick their arm in the car in an effort to show them the rocks they were selling. The customer was always looking for the biggest rocks for their money. Some people would legitly buying rocks that way. While others we soon discovered were looking for an easy way to rob us of our dope. Once we stuck our hands in the car to show the rocks the occupant would upwardly slap the bottom of our open hand causing the rocks to fly everywhere within the vehicle, the driver would immediately step on the gas pedal and take off with a free batch of rocks in his vehicle. The caveat was that these individuals could never show their faces on Jacqueline again because they would get severely assaulted. I've also seen people who would jump into the window as the car took off and I've seen some get drug.

So on this particular October night my homie Chris Fowler who was known as little C dog was there, Greg Jackson, and an older guy name Cliff was there. Cliff at that time was maybe twenty two. Chris was sixteen, and Greg and I were fifteen we were all just hanging in the alley. I believe Greg and Chris were selling weed. Cliff and I were trying to find a person coming to buy crack so we could find a way to flat out take their money or manipulate them out of it.

My intent was to get money so I could get some cocaine to roll a primo.

As I was in the alley waiting to participate I devious and criminal activities an older woman named Cookie approached me. "What's up little O.G." When she could see me, I replied, "Nothing just trying to make a few dollars." She then told me to come with her, and she went on to say that she had something for me.

Cookie was about 25 years old at the time. She was a rather tall woman with a taught voluptuous body. However, her face wasn't the prettiest sight to behold, once a man saw her body her face became insignificant Cookie led me to a nearby laundry room that was used by residents of the adjoining apartments. Once we were both inside she secured the door to the small room and commenced to put her hand down her pants to retrieve what appeared at first glance to be a small piece of balled up paper bag, I silently watched her as she unraveled the crumbled ball to reveal the contents. She had several pieces of rock cocaine and she took a small piece from one of the rocks that lay below the surface of that piece of paper bag that she casually held in her hand and put a piece of the tip of a small metal pipe that was fashioned out of a car antenna. Upon loading the pipe she passes it to me, and said, "Here hit this." I said, "No I'm cool, just give me a piece so I can role a primo." She was persistent about me hitting it, so against my better judgment I took that four inch pipe and put it between my lips as she stood in front of me coaching me with a lighter in hand on how I should smoke this unfamiliar method of smoking cocaine. She held the flame at the tip of the pipe and at her prompting she told me when to inhale. Once she held the lighter at the tip for a few seconds then she would pull the flame away and instruct me to pull it, (inhale,) I did, and she said hold it, and I did. I finally released that thick plume of smoke and within seconds an intense feeling of well being just consumed my mind and my body - I actually heard bells. I just stood there, I was able to talk but I didn't want to - that feeling was the best feeling I had ever experienced in my life. That was the beginning of what would prove to be an uphill battle with cocaine addiction.

The entire environment changed once I released that smoke and that intense rush overwhelmed me. Suddenly nothing mattered but my in the moment experience. When my high subsided I had a compelling urge to repeat the act of smoking cocaine on the pipe. I wanted to experience that state of euphoria again. What I didn't realize was that I would want to chase that high 24 hours a day, and that cocaine would become paramount in my life.

Each time I would inhale and exhale cocaine I would lose who I was as a person. My entire character would change and I moved away from the values characterized by being a human. I became numb in the sense that I didn't have any feelings, no compassion, and no empathy and definitely no love, my entire existence was predicated on getting high. The people that I once regarded as friends and family simply became objects, I only interacted with them because they served a purpose, and that purpose was me ultimately getting high. That meant hanging around them because they had money or drugs to contribute to feeding my insatiable drug habit.

I tried my best to keep my activities concealed from my poor mother, but I know she knew something was wrong because I became very withdrawn, and I would often isolate myself. The brief time that I would be at home was to eat, sleep and shower - interaction with my mother became very minimal. I would soon be back in the street and would return at two or three in the morning. I know my mom would be worried sick about me and my wants and desires. During this time period Jacqueline's drug trade was exclusively controlled by members of Sintown - (Tray-Five-Seven.)

The sudden influx of cocaine that was readily available to urban gang members created very interesting dynamics within the overall structure of the gang culture. Cocaine facilitated the divide amongst members who grew up together; suddenly cocaine came into the picture and suddenly two individuals who grew up with each other become rivals even though both are from the same gang.

There were certain members from my neighborhood who had a

monopoly on the cocaine trade within the parameters of the neighborhood. As this individual's economic success flourished so did his power and influence. As his power and influence increased he was able to hand pick certain guys from Sintown - (Tray - Five Seven) to be a part of his inner circle. You can imagine how fellow members who weren't part of the inner circle felt – jealous - thereby creating a rift between those who are part of the inner circle and those who are not. Of course those not part of the inner circle mask their jealousy by calling it something other than what it is, they would often come up with a way to assassinate certain member's character, i.e. calling certain members, snitches, punks or often exploiting some weakness. All in an effort to get other members to join their hate campaign.

In my neighborhood I remember a young guy they called Little Stone who was a very shrewd and seemingly successful drug dealer. Little Stone was short in stature - maybe 5'6" tall - he was a light skin, and extremely intelligent. His trade mark was his corduroy house shoes and his 501 Levi jeans. On any given day you could find him dressed in that apparel. He was very quiet, almost an intimidation type of silence. He was soft spoken and always appeared to be planning and calculating. Stone aligned himself with some of the Tray - Five Seven's elite hustlers: Dukie Damp, Cabbage, Old man - all three are brothers. Big C. Dog, and Sampson Baskerville - Sampson later founded the Crip gang in Pomona called West Side Mafia. These individuals were loyal members of Little Stone's lucrative drug selling venture. They functioned like a well oiled machine as they sold their product in various dope houses on Jacqueline Street and other parts of Pomona. Little Stone was even supplying dope to Sintown's rivals Pomona Islands (4-5-6 Bloods) Little Stone developed a working relationship with one of 4-5-6's high ranking members - Tom Slick.

The cocaine trade made it possible to secure surpluses of weapons, high priced vehicles which enabled the Crips and Bloods to branch out of their neighborhoods and into other states, thus maximizing their profits.

My appetite for cocaine continued to become increasingly larger I had to figure out a way to feed that insatiable monkey that was quickly growing into a guerilla. Each time I took a hit of cocaine I moved further and further away from my true character.

I remember Charles Harris (A.K.A. Charlie Mac) and I would often do things that could've gotten us seriously hurt and even killed in order to continue to feed our cocaine habit. Charles Harris at that time was twenty two years old seven years my senior. Charlie Mac is a well respected member of Sintown - (Tray - Five Seven,) his younger brother's nickname is Drack, he was also around during the Jacqueline days. I remember one particular night Charlie Mac and I went into the window of one of Little Stone's dope houses. We had knowledge of the fact that this particular apartment was raided by the police earlier that day, but a lot of the customers weren't aware of that. Back then the customer would simply knock on the sliding glass window which had a curtain behind it so they wouldn't know who they are purchasing from. When someone knocked we would slide the window back slightly and ask what they needed. They would specify their purchase desire and hand the money to us before even receiving the product. They did that because they knew that this was a bonifide crack house. But what they didn't know on this particular night was that two cocaine addicts were manning the window. So we lay in wait in the dark in a virtually empty apartment waiting for a victim. Suddenly we hear a car pull up to the curb just in front of the apartment window, then we hear the rickety noise of an old car door being opened then abruptly closed. Less than one minute later we hear an eager almost impatient tap on the window. I slide the window open slightly being extremely careful to conceal my identity as well as my voice. In my best disguised voice I uttered the words, "What you need?" I heard the low pitched voice reply, "Give me a five - O" before he completed that sentence he handed me a fifty dollar bill, I instructed him to hold on as I closed the window. Meanwhile Charles Harris and I made our escape through the side window while the customer patiently waited for my return. Of course we were gone with the wind and off to buy some dope so we could get high.

As my addiction continued to progress I was tasked with keeping my addiction concealed from my fellow gang members of Tray - Five Seven which was challenging to say the least. Around my homies I had to maintain my gang image while inwardly I knew I was completely out of character.

For many addicted to cocaine one of the tell tale signs of addiction is a decline in personal appearance and hygiene. If an individual was known for being meticulously neat and well groomed, then suddenly he appears unkempt and disheveled that is a huge red flag that points to cocaine addiction. To an individual addicted to cocaine appearance doesn't matter anymore, eating properly doesn't matter, getting sufficient sleep doesn't matter, all that matters is getting high.

I made painstaking efforts to maintain my personal appearance so as not to be perceived as a "crack head." The truth of the matter is I was a crack head. Keep in mind that in the Black community smoking crack was frowned upon, especially within gang culture.

I managed to keep it concealed from most of my fellow gang members, albeit there were a few that knew of my addiction as they were addicted as well.

I kept my addiction hidden from the main drug distributors at that time, so much so that they would give me drugs to sell on consignment. Little Stone and Dukie Damp would give me at least 200 dollars worth of crack and instructed me to bring them a fifty dollar return. I was able to discipline myself enough to refrain from smoking up all the product on maybe the first two occasions, on the third and forth package I was issued while my intentions were good however my addiction quickly overshadowed all intentions other than getting high. I would always go back down to the spot (apartment where drugs were being sold) and offer an excuse to Dukie Damp as to why I didn't have the fifty dollars that I owed. I would often say I had to throw it because the police were coming, and time and time again Dukie Damp would give me another 200 dollars worth of crack and demand I return fifty. He was always cool about the whole issue; after all he was dealing with kilos of cocaine at that time. Dukie Damp received his moniker as a result of him selling Sherm (P.C.P.) before the crack epidemic. In my area Sherm had several different street names, wet, loop, water, butt naked, and dukie stick, were some of the colorful adjectives to describe P.C.P. So Dewayne Damper was aptly referred to as Dukie Damp which was a clever play on words because Sherm was referred to as Dukie and wet - hence Dukie Damp fit perfectly being that his real last name was Damper.

I ended up smoking up the dope Dukie gave me. I was determined to uphold my image while at the same time maintain a constant channel for me to continue to get high. So I thought of a plan, a plan that I thought was fool proof.

My plan was to use any unsuspecting person who came through the alley to buy dope as the fall guy. I would make up a fictitious scenario that someone robbed me at gun point for my drugs after I showed him the drugs under the assumption that he wanted to purchase crack. I would pick someone and pretend that the individual returned a few days later and I would approach the individual at gun point. I put the plan in motion by alerting Dukie Damp that someone had robbed me for my dope in the alley. I remember this particular night clearly, I was inside the spot when Dukie came in with a paper bag full of small caliber hand guns, I remember telling him to give me one because someone had just robbed me. He handed me a .22 revolver from the bag that he held in his hand. He inquired about who robbed me and I stated I didn't know him, but I know his face if I see him again. Armed with the information that I was robbed everyone in the spot gathered their weapons and went to the alley in search of this unknown character who allegedly robbed me.

I executed my plan the following night, I was walking through the apartment court yard on Jacqueline Street and I saw an older man with broad shoulders, standing about 5' 11", dark skin with a 1" afro. I motioned toward this unfamiliar man with my revolver pointed in his direction, and I said; "Man why did you take my dope?" With a surprised and puzzled look on his face he raised his hands and said; "What are you talking about, don't shoot me please, don't kill me!" I then fired two shots to the side of him; I intentionally tried to miss him. I then turned around and took off running to ensure I wouldn't get apprehended by the police if they happened to be called. I thought nothing of that incident, and I didn't expect to ever see that guy again. I went on with my drug selling ventures in order to continue getting high.

Approximately two weeks after I pulled the gun on that guy that I didn't know Little C. Dog and myself were in the alley on this late October cold and gloomy night. I recall that I was wearing a beige colored trench with a black umbrella and a .25 caliber automatic hand gun in my pocket. Little C. Dog and I were both trying to sell our dope. As we patiently wait for a customer to pull up in the alley Little C. Dog and I engage in idle conversation, then suddenly a blue primer Pinto model car pulls into the entrance of the alley. As the car slowly makes its way through the alley young C. Dog and myself eagerly run up to the car in an effort to compete for the potential sell. As I briefly glanced at the driver of the vehicle I made a mental note of her identity it was Dukie Damp's (Dewayne Damper's) sister Mildred Damper. I could not make out who the passenger was because of the poor lighting in the alley. I would soon find out who the passenger was. Although we motioned to the vehicle the car continued to drive slowly past us and into the neighboring carport. Little C. Dog and I foolishly follow the car into the carport. We stand by as the car parks, and our focus is on the driver, we are expecting the driver to roll the window down. However, to our surprise the passenger door slowly opens and a towering man emerges from the vehicle holding what appears to be a M - 16 (.233 caliber clip fed assault rifle.) I hear him say as he points the weapon in my direction "Is that Dillinger? Let me see your face!" My face was obscured by the umbrella that I was holding. As he utters these words I put my hand in my pocket in an attempt to fire a shot from my .25 automatic at him; I point the weapon at him which was concealed in my pocket and squeezed the trigger! To my surprise the gun was on safety! I thought I was a dead kid in that moment. I instantly dropped the umbrella while Chris (Little C. Dog) silently looked on, and I took off running. By the grace of God not one shot was fired and I'm still alive to write about that situation. I can only attribute my survival to divine intervention, because he had all the opportunity in the world to kill me. I'm thankful that the gun was on safety because had I fired a shot at him, it more than likely wouldn't have disabled him, which probably would have given him justification to kill me. I would have fired one shot and turned to start running, and he would have opened fire before I got turned around. I would have lost my life at fifteen years old all behind my addiction being out of control. The guy who pulled the M - 16 on me was the same guy that I shot at and used as a fall guy regarding the made up robbery scenario. I later found out that his name was Ricky Malloy and he was an older member of the gang I was from, I was just so young I didn't know him.

Shortly after this incident I committed another crime with that .25 automatic hand gun that I had in my pocket on that night, and I was subsequently arrested - or should I say rescued - and sent back to the California Youth Authority to serve what would prove to be close to 3 years (2 years 9 months.)

I never saw Ricky Malloy after that night, however, in an ironic twist in the year 2000 I was about to enter a liquor store and before I could enter a gentleman who appeared to be weathered by heavy drug use approached me and said; "Hey Dillinger, do you have a dub?" Again a dub is street language for a 20 dollar rock of cocaine. I replied, "Yes, wait until I come out of the store." As I go into the store I'm puzzled as to who this individual is, and what's even more concerning is how he knew my nickname. So all the while I'm in the store my subconscious mind is at work trying to figure out who this guy is. He looks familiar, I just can't place where I know him from, then it dawns on me! Ricky Malloy! I couldn't believe it. The guy who could have killed me when I was fifteen years old is in my midst fifteen years later. I exit the store and approached him, and I say; "Wow! Ricky Malloy! You could've killed me that night." He replied as I handed him a twenty dollar rock in exchange for twenty dollars, "I was going to, but I knew you were just a baby!" I told him that I was young and stupid, and I apologized to him for pulling a gun on him. I motioned to give him a hug as a gesture of my apology and he was receptive to my forgiving embrace.

Fortunately for me I'm able to be alive to write about my unfortunate experiences. There are many who aren't as fortunate who either lost their lives or took a life during the cocaine epidemic. There are people who are still in prison right now for killing their own mother behind her not giving up money so that her son could continue to smoke crack, people lost their lives behind getting robbed for their dope. The cocaine epidemic played a huge part in the perpetuation of urban genocide.

The cocaine epidemic also opened the door for mass incarceration.

As a result of the cocaine epidemic it is estimated that 4.2 million people around the world were experimenting with the use of cocaine. It's estimated that in 1985 There were approximately 9,750 emergency room visits to the hospital due to cocaine related medical issues and by 1986 that number increased to a staggering 13,938; this made way for a generation of crack babies.

In 1989 an influx of court cases saturated the court rooms which gave rise to increased prison populations. Due in part to the disparity in drug laws minorities were receiving stiffer prison sentences than their white counterparts. For example, minorities would get 5 years for possession of 5 grams of crack, while our white counterparts would get the same 5 years for possessing 5 hundred grams of cocaine. The terms crack versus cocaine were racially biased in nature and used as a strategy to create the climate of mass incarceration for minorities.

In 1989 it was reported that 1 in 4 Black males ages 20-29 were either in jail or prison, or on parole or probation, by 1995 that number went to 1 in 3, giving support to the fact that the United States has the highest incarceration rate in the world.

The urban genocide is being perpetuated in America's jails and prisons in a similar vein to free society.

42

The Soledad Scandal

The California Training Facility commonly referred to as Soledad State Prison can be found in the Salinas Valley nearest the city of Soledad. Built in 1946 to help with overcrowding at San Quentin State Prison the facility was originally named Soledad State Prison and was renamed C.T.F. in late 1960.

Soledad was the first of the men's prisons built after the war (World War II.) One of the main qualities was its pleasant physical atmosphere. Fences and gun towers substituted for granite walls made prison life more bearable. Soledad cells equipped with windows that the occupant could open and close, spacious and well equipped libraries, gyms, acceptable food and more relaxed discipline, and a broad selection of vocational training and group counseling programs created a relatively friendly atmosphere more prone to rehabilitative treatment.

In the 1970's the facility began to take a turn when George Jackson became a resident at Soledad.

George Lester Jackson (September 23, 1941 - August 21, 1971) was an African American author, while serving a sentence for armed robbery in 1961; Jackson became involved in revolutionary activity and co-founded the Maoist - Marxist Black Guerrilla Family. In 1970 he was charged along with two other Soledad brothers, with the murder of prison guard John Vincent Mills in the aftermath of a prison fight between a Black inmate and a white inmate on Soledad's administrative segregation unit (O wing hole) recreation yard. The white officer who was manning the yard gun tower shot and killed the Black inmate during the physical altercation with a white inmate.

As retaliation for the incident in O - wing, Officer John Vincent Mills was thrown off the third tier to his death in Y - wing (A housing unit at Soledad Central Facility). Corrections officer Mills was the first officer at Soledad to lose his life in the line of duty.

The same year (1970) George Jackson published Soledad Brother; the prison letters of George Jackson is a combination of autobiography and manifesto addressed to a Black American audience. The book became a best seller and earned Jackson personal fame.

George Jackson and other revolutionary activist laid the foundation for the para military prison gang Black Guerrilla Family. In fact Soledad State Prison became headquarters, if you will, for the B.G.F. Sources say that the B.G.F. was a powerful and intimidating presence at Soledad. So much so that the officers in the housing units often turned a blind eye to the illicit activities for fear of being attacked or even killed by a B.G.F. member. Their activities included selling of drugs, extortion and other forms of criminal activity. I've talked to several people who were at Soledad during the 70's and 80's and they tell me that Soledad was a very violent place.

During the height of the Crip and Blood era Soledad was exceptionally violent as rivals often attacked one another. It's been said that back in the 80's Soledad housed an influx of Bloods. Crips were generally housed in dual vocational Institution (Tracy.) Soledad housed medium and maximum security inmates in the 80's which made the violence level very high. Back then the window of opportunity for lifers to go home was closed, and there was very little hope of ever getting out of prison.

Back then the mindset was "make the best of prison life because prison was the end of the road for lifers". Of course in today's time that paradigm has shifted for some. I say some because there are still segments of the prison population that don't particularly care to be in the free world even though the opportunity is available to them, they prefer to acquiesce to a life of prison, and follow the dictates of prison politics. I don't understand this mindset, nor do I subscribe to it, yet I'm aware that this thought pattern exists. I see the results based on their conduct every day.

I arrived here at Soledad C.T.F. on July 29, 2015. When I was processed in I was assigned to F-wing (Housing Unit.) Traditionally F-wing or Fox wing as it's referred as, housed the incorrigible inmates. I've been told by people who were here in the 80's that F-wing always housed some of the worst inmates. My experience with Fox wing has shown me that to a degree that theory is true. Since I've been here I've witnessed extreme drug activity, people frequently consuming prison made alcohol, and other unmentionable illicit activity.

The issues that plagued F-wing upon my arrival at Soledad were pervasive in other wings throughout the facility F-wing inmates who were participating in unsavory activity in most cases showed very little discretion. Aside from the small percentage of people who participated in behaviors that would keep them in prison, Soledad had a lot of inmates who were doing what's required to secure their freedom, e.g. staying out of trouble, participating in various rehabilitative programs, and setting a positive example for others to follow.

For the most part when I arrived Soledad was an ideal facility to do your time and ultimately put yourself in position to go home. There were very few negative incidents such as fights, and riots, we may experience a one on one fist fight every now and then, and they were generally isolated situations.

Although California prisons historically have been racially divided, meaning that each race generally sticks with its own race. For the most part all races at Soledad were respectful towards one another and there was no racial tension - covert or overt amongst the races. But for a small percentage of inmates that were adamant about persisting in criminal activity - everyone else seemed to be focused on the big picture - going home!

None the less, Soledad's relaxed environment abruptly shifted to one of violence, deceit, corruption, and racial hostility.

The following is a narrative outlined by the administration here at Soledad; it depicts what happened on the yard one Sunday morning.

The following situation would prove to be the beginning of an ongoing war against two opposing factions (Hispanics.)

On Sunday, August 05, 2018 at approximately 1048 hours, a riot involving approximately 85 inmates from the Bulldogs, Sureños Mexican Mafia and Paisa (Mexican Nationals) security threat groups occurred on C yard. A code 3 response was initiated. Staff utilized chemical and impact munitions to quell the incident. Since the incident on August 5th 2018, Facility C has received information from independent sources regarding the possibility of an existing threat including individual threat assessments, searching and interviews. Following C.D.C.R. unlock protocol, on Thursday August 16th, 2018 Facility C began an incremental release of 8 inmates in the morning and 8 inmates in the afternoon release based on identified affected inmates with low risk assessments. On Friday August 17th, 2018 Facility C will continue on incremental release of 8 inmates in the morning only, based on identified affected inmates with low risk threat assessments. As a result Facility C will continue a modified program on the STG II Bulldogs, Sureños, STG I Mexican Mafia and Paisa (Mexican Nationals) with the exception of the affected inmates on the incremental release.

This situation was sparked by a dispute over the telephones that inmates use on the yards. Allegedly a Mexican National used a telephone that was designated as a Bulldog phone. In prison most of the real estate is racially divided, or divided according to various gang ideologies. Shortly after it was discovered by the members of the Bulldogs that their phone was being used by an unauthorized party an attack ensued. When this fight broke out Sureños came running to the aide of their Mexican Nationals, and based on eyewitness account the Sureños ran to the scene in what appeared to be a throng of hundreds. Although correctional officers documented in their report 85 inmates, eyewitness accounts claimed there were at least 200 who ran to the altercation to assist the Mexican Nationals.

This incident was a manifestation of the internal disdain that had been brewing in the minds and hearts of the Sureños. When the Mexican Nationals initiated that altercation with the Bulldogs behind the yard phone, that incident served as a perfect opportunity to demonstrate that they are a force to be reckoned with.

The then F-14's successfully broke away from their subordinate relationship with Nuestra Familia and became independent. It was in 1986 that they adopted the name Bulldogs. The Bulldogs lack infrastructure and visible leadership that's what makes them extremely dangerous.

In a similar vein, the Sureños are the foot soldiers of the prison based group Mexican Mafia. The Sureños street gang are linked to the Mexican Mafia both in prison and in free society.

The Mexican Mafia was founded in Tracey State Prison (D.V.I) in 1956, shortly thereafter the cornerstone members were transferred to San Quentin. Although their numbers were few, they managed to establish a broad power base by leveraging four components, fear, violence, extortion, and intimidation. For example, they would often misuse the Hispanics from Northern California; they viewed them as "farmers" who didn't measure up to the standard of toughness set by those from the greater Los Angeles area, the native origin of most of the Mexican Mafia members is Los Angeles.

Being that Mexican mafia members viewed Northern Hispanics in an unfavorable light, they would often misuse them , they would take cigarettes from the Northern Hispanics cells, and on one occasion they stole a pair of tennis shoes from a Northern Hispanic. This situation prompted the Northern Hispanics to band together; to form the prison vanguard known as Nuestra Familia to defend themselves from the exploits of the Mexican Mafia. The shoe theft served as the starting point of the persistent war between the two factions: Nuestra Familia and Mexican Mafia. The incident was later dubbed the "Shoe War."

Soledad's peaceful and relaxed atmosphere was met with an abrupt paradigm shift due in part to the ramifications of a landmark case filed by Pelican Bay State Prison SHU (Security Housing Unit) prisoners Todd Ashker and Danny Troxell.

When the case was filed in 2012 more than 500 prisoners had been isolated in the security housing unit at Pelican Bay for over 10 years and 78 had been there for more than 20 years, they spent 22½ to 24 hours in a cramped concrete windowless cell, and denied telephone calls, physical contact with visitors, vocational, recreational, and educational programming. Hundreds of other prisoners throughout California were held in similar conditions.

The seeds of this victory are in the unity of the prisoners in their peaceful hunger strike of 2011, that courageous and principled protest galvanized support on both sides of the prison walls ultimately leading to legal victory.

Although many residents of Pelican Bay's SHU had to endure extreme conditions such as continuous isolation and sensory deprivation which caused mental issues in many of the men, the Mexican Mafia members there managed to defy the harsh riggers of that environment and maintain the presence of mind enough to call shots from deep within the bowels of Pelican Bay SHU.

These men were controlling the California prison system from the confines of Pelican Bay SHU. One member who debriefed admitted to officials that he was conducting business right under the Department of Corrections noses, he further admitted that he was making at least 60,000 a year, he admitted to taking care of his family and putting his children through college all the while under the watchful scrutiny of prison officials. These men ingeniously circumvented Pelican Bays once air tight security policies and procedures.

We must not lose sight of the fact that although members of this well known prison gang were essentially running an enterprise while in prison, the fact remains that their enterprise was illegal, and the entire thought patterns required to put their diabolical plots and plans in motion were deceptive and criminal; which speaks to the issue of rehabilitation. These individuals by no fault of their own were not afforded the opportunity to participate in any form of rehabilitation while housed in the security housing unit. No therapy groups were offered, no educational classes, and no vocational training classes were offered to these men housed in this isolated setting. Albeit these individuals had the free will to rehabilitate themselves by virtue of other means, i.e. religion, self reflection, and self correction of negative character traits, many of the men acquiesced to rigid and sterile vestiges of extreme isolation and sensory deprivation.

Studies have shown that being isolated and deprived of human contact is psychologically damaging; some of these men have been subjected to those extreme conditions for over ten years, some even twenty.

When the landmark case was implemented in 2016 it marked the end of the old prison validation process, in times past inmates were validated as prison gang members for simply having a guerrilla etched on a cup purchased from commissary, or being found in possession of Aztec drawings. I talked to one inmate here at Soledad and he informed me that he created a collage which contained a picture of George Jackson, Malcolm X, and Martin Luther King and he was sent to Ad Seg, pending investigation for possible affiliation to the Black Guerrilla Family.

It was in 2016 when Soledad received its first group of inmates who were released from the SHU a result of the new agreement pursuant to the lawsuit filed by inmates Todd Ashker and Danny Troxell.

They were placed in a facility that traditionally was a place where everyone was doing what they needed to do to position themselves for their imminent or eventual release, then out of nowhere the "higher ups" decided that it would be a great idea to place inmates who were entrenched in warped criminal thinking patterns, who weren't afforded the opportunity to participate in any rehabilitation programs, and these individuals were arbitrarily dropped off here at Soledad. The move was arbitrary in the sense that there was no provision for these inmates to be acclimated back into general population after being under the harsh conditions of Pelican Bay's SHU Program, or one of the many SHU facility's within California's prison system, e.g. Corcoran and Tehachapi. In times past when an inmate was released from the SHU the inmate had to be housed in a maximum security (180 design) facility in order to go through a readjustment process, however that practice is antiquated in C.D.C.R's view. It's not hard to figure out if you take an inmate who has not participated in any form of rehabilitation and who is still an active prison gang member and you place this individual in a facility were inmates have earned their right to be there based on their rehabilitative efforts, it's safe to say based on empirical evidence that these few individuals will be like a cancer that will consume the minds and hearts of those who are subjugated by these prison gang member dictates.

Case in point C.D.C.R. requires that long term inmates go to what's known as a reentry release. Why? Because these guys that have served over ten years in prison have become socially handicapped and they would not function properly in free society without first ted to the society first.

It stands to reason that if C.D.C.R. requires that inmates who have served lengthy prison re-entry facilities, the same principle should be applied to inmates being released from the segregated housing units after serving lengthy terms coupled with isolation and issues.

Instead C.D.C.R. knowingly and willingly opted to release special needs inmates into facilities where rehabilitation is the bedrock of the prison.

The consequence of C.D.C.R's choice to allow these inmates to be housed here at Soledad without gradually acclimation back into the prison's general population has created a powder keg environment.

Now suddenly active prison gang members who were once segregated from the general population of the prison because of their validation to well known prison gangs along with their unwavering allegiance to their structure have abruptly been allowed to go back to the same facilities that initially deemed them a security threats to the facility. Essentially these inmates were placed in the SHU due in part to the negative power and influence that they held within the particular organization.

Along with the arrival of certain inmates who were released from the SHU came a pronounced racial divide. The rapport that blacks once had with certain inmates of other races suddenly became estranged and distant. It should be further noted that black inmates did not initiate this divide.

On Tuesday, October 16, 2018 at approximately 0825 hours, multiple, simultaneous disturbances occurred on Facility C involving security threat group (STG) II Fresno Bulldogs, STG I Mexican Mafia and STG Sureños and Paisas (Mexican Nationals.) The inmate population was placed on modified program. On November 16th, 2018, it was determined that STG II white non-specific inmates were added to the list of affected inmates due to their involvement in incidents at two separate institutions. On December 6th, 2018 Woods (white disrupted prison group) and Out Law Motorcycle gang will remain on modified program. On December 14th, affected inmates will be provided showers. Health care request forms (c.d.c.r.7362) will be picked up daily at the cell by health care staff and documented in the log book. All ADA (American Disability Act) accommodation shall be met.

This incident was a well thought out and organized attack of all the Bulldogs in every wing here at Soledad. On queue at the sound of an alarm going off at medical which meant one officer from every wing deployed to the alarm, this served as an ideal for everyone in every wing to attack the Bulldogs. Checkmate! The plan was a success; staff were in a state of confusion as they were unprepared to deal with such an unprecedented and intricate scheme.

This incident prompted the removal of all Bulldogs throughout the general housing units where Sureños co-existed and placed in housing units isolated from Southern Hispanics. The incident was| also a way for Southern Hispanics to attempt to solidify their power base, in hopes to instill fear in the minds and hearts of inmates and staff alike. In my opinion that was part of their objective.

There are currently throngs of Southern Hispanics (Sureños) housed here at Soledad they out number (the black population by at least three to one. The Sureños also share an allegiance with white inmates, specifically the well known prison gang Arian Brotherhood. The Mexican Nationals are aligned with the Sureños as well. In time of war these allied groups will join forces with African American inmates, for African American men because historically within California prisons the consensus has always been black inmates are objects of hatred by all races.

Once again no one was given a rule violation report for the widespread facility attack of the Bulldogs by Southern Hispanics; however both groups were placed on a lengthy lockdown which didn't end for Southern Hispanics for another eight months.

During the interim of the lockdown neither group was allowed to visit with family, they were not allowed quarterly packages nor canteen (commissary.) Yet they still managed to circumvent most of the restrictions. Having a deep sense of compassion and empathy many of the black's assisted the Southern Hispanic's by allowing members of their group to place money on black inmate accounts in order to go the facility commissary for them, many of the black's allowed the Southern Hispanic's to order quarterly packages in their names of course charged a nominal fee for service. The point is, even though we knew that the political racial divide existed between us we were willing to forgo those prison politics to help relieve their suffering in the interest of being humane.

The groups that were locked down were designated by the administration as security threat groups. These validated members have been placed into two separate and distinct classifications;

Security Threat Group 1 and Security Threat Group II.

Per C.D.C.R. California Code of Regulations manual (Title 15) Security threat group I consists of groups, gangs and or historically based prison gangs that C.C.C.R. has determined to be the most severe threat to the security of the institutions and communities based on a history and propensity for violence and or influence over other STG affiliates.

Security threat group II consists of other groups or gangs such as street gangs or disruptive groups comprised of members and associates who may be determined to be in a role to the more dominant STG-I groups.

Mexican Mafia members are classified as STG-I's and their subordinates Sureños are classified as STG-II's.

The title 15 also states under the subheading security threat group behavior or activity that C.D.C.R. inmates shall not participate in STG activity or behavior, and a disciplinary matrix is outlined which highlight specific behavior or activity displayed by STG members that will not be permitted within the facility. For example, the disciplinary matrix says an inmate who is a valid member of an STG is prohibited from acting in a leadership role and displaying behavior to organize and control other offenders within the STG. Although I've noted that most of the operations conducted by STG members is highly clandestine, however. I've witnessed on several occasions members of prison gangs walking around the facility visibly escorted by groups of at least four body guards. Staff witnesses this activity and turn a blind eye to it. Furthermore, participating in group exercise is forbidden on general population yards, yet on any given day during yard group exercises are taking place by STG members en masse. By all outward appearances staff here at Soledad are working in concert with these groups by allowing their para-military activity to take place.

I believe C.D.C.R. officials have a vested interest in the fostering and covertly encouraging the recent violent behavior that has been taking place as of late. The reason I hold sway to that opinion is because for decades California Department of Corrections made billions of dollars of[7] of the unfortunate plight of inmates who were serving time that was grossly disproportionate to their crime, but in light of drastic changes in law many are now being released. Th;se recent mass releases in my opinion are jeopardizing the job security that prison officials once touted as having. In light of the most recent law changes which affords many who once thought they would never get out of prison, the opportunity to go home. Do you think prison officials are delighted about this notion? Of course not, so they strategically devised a way to lobby for more money and more staff. They do this by allowing prison gang members to wield their power and influence within various prison yards, thus creating racial tension, racial divides, and ultimately racial riots in which someone is seriously injured or killed. All the while prison officials could care less about who gets injured or killed as a result of racial prison politic, their main concern is amassing more wealth, at the expense of shed inmate blood. This big chess game set up by in my opinion only contributes to the ongoing perpetuation of urban genocide.

Declaration of Hate

According to a recent report from the Southern Poverty Law Center, hate groups in the United States have continued to surge in the Trump era, and it has been reported that the President himself has helped to mainstream hate by "fueling fears of a white minority country." The Alabama based SPLC- is touted as one of the longest standing and widely cited anti - hate organizations, counted 1,020 hate groups in 2018, up 7% from the previous year.

Officials say this represented an all time high since the SPLC began counting hate groups, in 2011, when the far rights angry reaction to the Obama Presidency was peaking. Although many groups are objects of hatred for various reasons, the reports indicate that in every tally of hate crimes Blacks are the most frequent victims. Why are Blacks across the county hated simply for being Black?

Why are people of color frequently the objects of hatred, discrimination, and often violence? To answer that age old question we must go back in history. During slavery, it was common practice to demonize Blacks in order to instill psychological inferiority in the mind of slaves. Strategic brainwashing was reinforced by the continuous mistreatment of slaves in an attempt to solidify the docile and inferior mindset. For example, if a person is told they are stupid, ugly, and worthless, eventually they will internalize those degrading labels, and their conduct will be the manifestation of what they have decided is true about who they are. They will then behave consistent with the labels heaped upon them.

I believe that the opposite is true regarding a mindset of superiority. There are people who actually behave in a manner consistent with being superior to African Americans. Why? They are conditioned psychologically to think they are superior to Blacks based on the premise that Blacks are ignorant, lazy, prone to violence, uncouth, and loud. Although these traits may be true for some) Blacks, I can apply that same standard to any race of people and I'm sure those traits can be found. So the bottom line is as human beings there are good and bad people, rich and poor people, educated, and uneducated people in every race. Yet for some reason Blacks seem to be viewed as the lowest form of human existence.

Fredrick Douglass became one of the first Black role models as a result of his self imposed rise from essentially nothing to what would prove to be the forerunner of Black intelligence in America.

Prior to his laudable conquests, it's appalling to glance back at history and be reminded that during slavery people had to endure forced labor, and mothers in some cases had to look on helplessly while their infant children were used as bait for alligators. The slave existence was less than human.

When the slaves were freed from slavery in 1865 before the Civil War ended, white society let Blacks know in no uncertain terms that they were not welcome as freed residents. I use the term residents because Blacks were by no means citizens, they were simply residents with no rights existing and trying to carve out their own economic niche in America's hate filled racially charged climate.

With very few economic opportunities Blacks were forced to become entrepreneurs and make a way out of no way - so to speak. That entrepreneurial drive and determination gave birth to people like Booker T. Washington, Madame C.J. Walker, W.E.B. Dubois and Marcus Garvey.

Yet despite best efforts, stereotype regarding Blacks always seemed to take center stage, always portrayed I news stories as victims, trouble makers, and members of the lowest level of human existence.

We as Black people seemed the exclusive forerunners of the arts, entertainment and civil right movements.

Speaking of civil rights, we as Black people will never forget the segregation of the Jim Crow era when Southern States passed laws that excluded Blacks from enjoying equal basic human rights, the basic right to be treated fairly and with dignity and decency. Instead during the Jim Crow era Blacks were treated with utter distain. Signs that read "No Coloreds" were sprawled across America's landscape making it unequivocally clear that even though slavery officially ended in 1865, Blacks were still viewed as separate and unequal to the mainstream of American society.

Immediately after the Civil War ended, Southern States enacted "black codes" that allowed African American's certain rights, such as legalized marriage, ownership of property, and limited access to the courts, denying them right to testify against whites, to serve on juries or in state militias, vote, or start a job without approval of the previous employer. These codes were replaced in 1866 when recon construction began.

But after the failure of reconstruction in 1877, and the removal of

Black men from political offices, Southern States enacted a series of laws intended to circumscribe the lives of African Americans. Harsh contract laws penalized poor African Americans for crimes such as stealing a farm animal and vagrancy statues made it a crime to be unemployed. Many misdemeanors were treated as felonies, with harsh sentences and fines.

The Pig Laws stayed on the books for decades, and were expanded with even more discriminatory laws once the Jim Crow era began.

The 13th Amendment states that, "neither slavery nor involuntary servitude, except as a punishment for a crime where of the party shall have been duly convicted, shall exist within the United States or any other place subject to their jurisdiction."

Black codes intent and effect of compelling them to work in a labor economy based on low wages and debt. Black codes were part of a larger pattern of southern whites who were trying to suppress the new freedom of emancipated African American slaves, the freedmen. This period was the start of the convict based system.

Those systemic practices that were well thought out strategies to legally use Black people as slaves, and make money at the same time.

That is exactly what the modern day United States industrialized prison complex represents - modern day slavery and mega profits under the clever guise of public safety.

In fact the United States prison population has sky rocketed past 2 million, with millions more awaiting a judicial disposition in the local county jails. The recent studies of prison expansion resoundingly speak to the persistent disparities in sentencing according to race. Prison populations have persistently remained disproportionately African American and Latino with longer sentences being imposed for non - violent drug offenses, and aggressive campaigns aimed at criminalizing young people. Meanwhile, the number of children left orphaned in the wake of the United States scheme to mass incarcerate continues to elevate.

State and private corporations resonate with the history of slavery and mark a level of human bondage unparalleled in our recent epoch.

Scholars and activists have plunged into an examination of the historical origins of radicalized slavery as a coercive labor farm and social system in an attempt to explain the huge increase in mass incarceration in the United States since the end of World War II. These studies have been essential in outlining the bridge between racism and slavery post emancipation, and linking the expansion of the industrialized prison complex and mechanized labor to the destructive effects of deindustrialization.

The clear connections between racism and the global economy called mass incarceration occupies a phase along the lines of unfree labor thunderously speaks to chattel slavery.

The unrelenting efforts to criminalize people of color are not a new tactic. During slavery various labels were thrust upon slaves in a sick attempt to cover up their own demonic and immorally twisted thinking. For example, slave women were often described by slave owners as hyper sexual meaning that they wanted sex all the time; this was an ingenious way of justifying their inward sexual desires for slave women. The same labels were placed on slave men; they were viewed as animals with uncontrolled sexual desires and pronounced endowment. This was justification for slave owner's wives to have sex with black slaves. The same holds true of the criminalization of a segment of people, namely Blacks and Latinos, society can justify their acts by making money from the downtrodden members of our society - a way to ease the conscience.

Our conscience serves as our moral compass alerting us when we have made a bad choice morally. If our conscience is calibrated properly it will give us an accurate reading - so to speak. Our conscience will prod at us or strike us when we have made a bad choice. Normally if ones conscience is healthy the person will feel shame or guilt and sorrow - all designed for us to ultimately repent from our wrong doings. However if we ignore the warnings or prodding's of our conscience it can become seared. To illustrate, think of how certain farm animals are branded with an extremely hot branding iron for identification purposes. Once that wound heals the scar tissue develops and that area becomes devoid of feeling. The same holds true with our conscience, if we ignore its prodding's it becomes devoid of feeling – desensitized it doesn't work.

I submit that the powers that be in American society have allowed their consciences to become inoperable long ago.

Case in point, a 14 year old black boy was arrested in Alcolu South Carolina in 1944. He was accused of killing two white girls, 11 year old Betty and Mary age 7 whose bodies were found near the house where the boy and his parents lived. At that time, all members of the jury were white. During his trial he always carried his Bible in his hands as he proclaimed his innocence. The trial lasted 2 hours and the sentence was dictated 10 minutes later, he was sentenced to death!

The boy's parents were not allowed in the court room, and subsequently expelled from that city after the trial.

Before the execution George spent 81 days in prison without being able to see his parents, he was held in solitary 80 miles from his city, he was held alone without anybody to talk to. He was electrocuted with 5380 volts in his head. 70 years later, in 2014 his innocence was finally proven by a judge in South Carolina.

George Stinney Jr. was the youngest person to be sentenced to death in United States history.

Talk about damaged consciences, that story is the hallmark of pure hatred for Black people, and clear evidence that age was not a factor - being Black was concrete evidence, enough to yield a guilty verdict. The strategic criminalization of Black men continues to persist today. Another example of urban genocide.

Oppression Breeds Revolt

A study done by Stanford University provides the frame work which traces the earliest formations of African American gangs.

A gang is an interstitial group formed spontaneously, and then integrated through conflict. It is characterized by the following types of behavior: Meeting face to face, milling, milling through space as a unit, conflict and planning.

The result of this collective behavior is the development of traditional unreflective internal structure, esprit de corps, solidarity, morale, group awareness and attachment to territory.

African American gangs began to emerge in Los Angeles area during the 1920's which was in concordance with the large black population in the city. The gangs in existence at this time in history were not territorial. On the other hand, they were loose associations, unorganized, and rarely violent. Moreover, they did not employ monikers, graffiti, or various other gang characteristics to identify themselves. Gangs of the 20's and 30's were mainly composed of family members and friends, and they were involved only in very limited criminal actions.

In fact the main purpose of those criminal activities was to transmit a "tough guy" image and to provide an easy means of obtaining money.

During the 1920's and 1930's gangs such as the "Goodlows," "Kelley's," "Magnificents," "Driver Brothers," "Boozies," and the "Bloodgets, wandered the streets of Los Angeles. All of these gangs committed petty crimes in comparison to gangs today. The Boozies, for example consisted of brothers and their friends who engaged in prostitution and forgery. As the 1940's approached black gangs were beginning to grow in number. Gangs including "Purple Hearts," "31st Street," and "28th Street," emerged in this decade, and their activities were very similar to those gangs in the 20's and 30's. In addition to theft, prostitution and forgery, gangs of the 40's were involved in extortion and gambling. They were effective in forcing local merchants to pay the gangsters for protection which amounted to paying the gang not to rob the merchant's store.

The 1950's witnessed the arrival of car clubs, which included the "Low Riders," "Coasters," "Highwaymen," "Road Devils," "Businessmen," "Gladiators," "Slausons," "Rebel Rousers," "Hun's," "Watts Farmers," and "Blood Alley." These particular gangs were extremely protective of their territory; however they were not organized very well and did not consist of many members. The activities of the gangs remained the same in relation to previous decades. Any conflicts that did arise between gangs occurred when rival gang members found themselves in an enemy's territory. As was generally the case, each gang would gather its members together, meet in a deserted lot or park and physically fight to the end. The gang with the most people standing at the conclusion of the fight was declared the winner, and the losers would limp home and recover. Weapons such as chains, knives, and bats were used occasionally in these rival conflicts. These types of weapons are in stark contrast to the commonly used semi automatic handguns and AK-47's used in today's gang fights.

As the 1950's came to an end the next decade emerged, car clubs began to languish and more organized groups came to the fore front. The late 1960's was the site of the development of what would be one of the most violent and unlawful gangs in the history of Los Angeles, the Crips.

It all began with the creation of a small gang called "Baby Avenues" by two South Central Los Angeles High School students, Raymond Washington, and Stanley Williams, (Tookie.) These young men soon began referring to their gang as the Crib's which is thought to have eventually given rise to the current name of the South Central based gang, the Crips. Raymond and Tookie claimed to have started this particular gang as a means of protection against other gangs in the area who were committing various crimes.

The activities of the Crips originated on high school campuses throughout the Los Angeles area. Freemont High School was home for the "Eastside Crips" and the "Westside Crips " originated on the opposite side of the 110 Harbor freeway. In addition, another faction of Crips formed in the Compton area of Los Angeles County which came to be known as the Compton Crips.

Nearly a decade after the institution of this particular gang, the Crips had grown from a small Los Angeles gang to an organization with members spread across the State of California. Even previously established gangs such as Main Street Crips, Kitchen Crips, came to consolidate the Crip name into their gang set. Despite the fact that these gangs embraced the Crip name, they often remained independent and continued to have their own leadership and members.

Many of the Crip subsets were in conflict with one another due to the independent nature of several of the gangs. Thus the Crips had become just like the gang members they had once sought to protect themselves from - Crips had become gang bangers who terrorized their own neighborhoods.

During the early years of existence, Crips main activities included extortion of funds from non-gang members, theft and assault. The founders of the Crips gang both lost their affiliation with the gang close to a decade after its establishment. A rival gang member murdered Raymond Washington in 1979 and Tookie was incarcerated that same year on four counts of murder; subsequently was executed by the State of California after a long legal fight of actual innocence in 2005.

During the early 1970's several other African American gangs emerged in an effort to protect themselves from the many Crip gangs forming in the area. One of the most well known of these particular gangs is the Bloods, which came to be one of the most violent and unlawful African American gangs in Los Angeles.

The Blood's established themselves around the West Piru Street area in the Compton section of Los Angeles County. Sylvester Scott and Vincent Owens were the founders of the Bloods and this certain gang actually started out as "Compton Pirus." The swift expansion of the Bloods was aided by severe conflict between Compton Crips, and the Compton Pirus, in which the Pirus were greatly outnumbered and brutally crushed. The conflict brought several sets of the Pirus together, and Pirus subsequently joined forces with the Lueder's Park Hustlers, and the L.A Brims. In fact the Brims were quite fervent to join forces against the Crips, who had recently murdered one of their gang members. Various other gangs around the area who had been attacked or threatened in the past by the Crips were also eager to join forces against them, and these gangs were united under the Blood name. "Red" gangs in the Compton area refer to themselves as Pirus, and several other "red" gangs in that area such as Brims, Bounty Hunters, Swans, and Inglewood Family are known as Bloods. Those associated with Bloods are fairly well accredited for their "take no prisoners" attitude as well as for their merciless and violent behavior.

Prior to the 1980's Crips and Bloods had limited active participation in narcotics trafficking. However in 1983 African American Los Angles gangs seized upon the availability of narcotics, particularly crack as a means of income. Many of the gang members who became involved in the buying and selling of narcotics came from inner city areas where poverty and unemployment are a way of life. Gangsters could make anywhere from three hundred to five hundred dollars per day selling crack cocaine. Thus many became involved in that line of work.

The Crips and Bloods, although they are said to have evolved as protectors of their respective communities, I submit that these two inner city groups represent the birth of frustration, the birth of a gaping disconnect to societies often biased and systemically racist social norms, quite frankly. The Crips and Bloods represent the back lash of the oppressed urban youth and a never ending quest to establish identity and a sense of belonging.

Anytime another human being attempts to oppress another human being, one of two things will occur, one either gives up or submits to the oppressive and harsh treatment, or one becomes tired of the oppressive and harsh treatment and figures out a way to revolt against the treatment.

As for the Crips and Blood their revolt was directed towards each other. They didn't collectively come together to pro-socially combat the systemic racism that many young black urban youth were confronted with in the inner cities.

Instead their hatred was directed at other young black men who share their exact plight, young, poor, uneducated, and victims of racism and discrimination.

Many of the members of the Crips and Bloods were bright and industrious; however, their potential was channeled in the wrong areas. Many of them were great salesmen and entrepreneurs as it relates to selling drugs.

The same energy that was applied to selling illegal drugs could have been applied to going to school and educating themselves about legitimate business. They could've taken the exact same skills that was required to moving drugs and applied it to legally moving units in business. Instead many opted to persist in illegal activity only to face harsh consequences in the wake of their choice. Many fell victim to drug use, perpetual stints of incarceration, and many lost their lives from either gang violence, or getting robbed and killed as a result of a drug deal gone bad.

I would say maybe 20 percent of all gang members are able to wake from the destructive mindset and change the trajectory of their life before the devastating consequences of gang life bears fruit; life in prison or death.

When we revisit history we discover the truthfulness of the often revolting. Consequences of oppressing a segment of the human population, violence. One thing about human beings we have the ability to understand, reason, and we all have an ingrained desire to love and be loved, it's how Jehovah God made us. No one enjoys being mistreated... in fact; continuous mistreatment often causes a human being to rebel against the oppressive construct.

Nat Turner provides us with a classic narrative of history where oppression leads to revolt. Nat Turner's revolt was a slave rebellion that took place in Southampton County Virginia in August 1831, led by Nat Turner. Rebel slaves killed 55 to 65 people, at least 51 being white. The rebellion was put down within a few days, but Nat Turner survived in hiding for more than two months afterwards. The rebellion was effectively suppressed at Belmont Plantation on the morning of August 23, 1831.

Nat Turner's rebellion was one of the largest slave rebellions ever to take place in the United States, and it played an important role in the development of antebellum slave society. The images from Nat Turner's rebellion - of armed Black men roaming the country side slaying white men women and children - haunted white southerners and showed slave owners how valuable they were. Following the rebellion whites throughout the South were determined to prevent any further slave insurrections, and they tightened the already harsh slave codes to keep African Americans, slave and free, in a subservient position.

Nat Turner was born in 1800 into slavery in Southampton Virginia, about twenty miles from the North Carolina border. Turner's experience was typical of slaves on Southampton plantations. He had little freedom; he could not legally marry, own property, earn money or travel without his master's permission. He was forced to work long hard hours in the fields for meager rations of food and clothing, and if he refused he faced the whip or other punishment. Like many slaves Turner was sold several times to different masters. Each time he was forced to leave family and friends and move to a different plantation.

It was this brutal, demeaning system of slavery that Nat Turner sought to over throw. He sought not only his own freedom, but to dismantle the entire system of slavery and liberate African Americans from white tyranny.

Fast forward to 1966 the year the Black Panther Party was founded. The movement originally started under the name Black Panther Party for Self Defense. This revolutionary party was founded in Oakland California by Huey Newton and Bobby Seale. The party's original purpose was to patrol African American neighborhoods to protect residents from acts of police brutality. The Panthers eventually developed onto a Marxist revolutionary group that called for the arming of all African Americans, the exemption of African American from the draft and from all sanctions of so - called white America, the release of all African American's from jail, and payment of compensation to African American's for centuries of exploitation by white American's. At its peak in the late 1960's Panther members exceeded 2,000 and the organization operated chapters in major American cities.

The Panthers formed as a response to the social, economic, political, and oppressive elements that adversely affected African Americans of that era. They were sick and tired of police harassment, police brutality, and over all unfair and often inhumane treatment, such as a response to the oppression the Panther revolted.

The Race of Endurance

Being a Black man in today's hate filled and racially divided world is one of the most challenging things that a person of African descent has to grapple with not just sometimes, but daily.

Granted everyone in life experiences hurdles and obstacles in different forms - that's just part of the human condition. Conversely however, the African American males hurdles and obstacles just happen to be a lot harder to get past. I am aware that in life success or failure is a choice, but even in our attempts to succeed there are systemic structures in place to prevent us from obtaining success or to impede our success.

Throughout my life all of my misfortune was directly linked to the choices that I made, I take full responsibility for my actions. I do believe that although I chose to participate in unsavory activity that I knew would result in losing my liberty; I also believe that Blacks and Latino's are disproportionately punished by the judicial system. Using myself as example, I was convicted of 2nd degree murder which under legal statutes carries a maximum of 15 years to life, here is the caveat: under California's three - strike law if you have been convicted of a prior serious felony this would constitute a strike. I was convicted for 2nd degree robbery in 1991 and sentenced to 2 years 8 months in State Prison. I served time for this crime and was placed on parole. Keep in mind that I had no clue that in March of 1994 a three - strike you're out law would be enacted and suddenly the time that I served in 1991 would be grounds to re-punish me.

Now under the law my base term of 15 to life would have to be doubled due to my strike from 1991, and two additional years on top of the additional 15 years would be applied for having gone to prison on two separate commitments, plus an additional 5 years for committing a felony within what they call a "five year wash out period." By the time my sentencing hearing was over I received an additional 22 years worth of enhancements to my sentence. I left court with a whopping 37 years to life sentence. Sentencing disparity at its best! The vast majority of people who receive these draconian sentences just happen to be Black and Latino. In my view this is another clever scheme intended to strategically take you away from free society for lengthy periods of time. I've seen people who were struck out under the three strikes law serve more time than a person convicted for first and second degree murder, a third strike crime that would warrant a year in the county jail at best; yet the men here who have been locked up close to 25 years for a crime as trivial as stealing bologna from a supermarket where no violence was used and yet these individuals have served more time than someone who took a human life. First degree murder is punishable by 25 years to life, and many offenders have served 21 years and the parole board has deemed them parole ready (or suitable for parole,) many of these offenders are currently home. Meanwhile, the three-strike offender who didn't hurt anyone languishes in prison for 25 years before he is eligible to go to the parole board to be "considered" for parole. It's not hard to see the disparity in that illustration, and all too often blacks and Latino's are bearing the brunt of today's unfair "just us" system.

The intentional criminalization of certain segments of society who happen to be poor, uneducated, and often mentally ill, a misnomer used by those in positions of power in this country to hinder or completely lock out the down trodden from obtaining upward socio-economic mobility. The goal is to prevent certain groups of people from being independent financially and dependent on those who are in positions to affect change.

I don't want to be misunderstood and classified as prejudice, racist, or pro-black. I am neither of these labels; however I am aware that the aforementioned mind sets exist in those I encounter on a daily basis here in prison. I can unequivocally say that these diseased mind sets exist in free society to a large degree. Although I don't subscribe to any form of biased views toward any race of people, I am aware of the mistreatment of Blacks that has taken place during slavery right up to the present. My position is to point out the diabolical and sadistic forms of mistreatment that has been aimed at people of color long after the end of slavery.

This begs the question, can African Americans be racist? First we must understand the concept of race. Race is defined as a concept of society that is a genetic significance behind human variations in skin color that transcends outward appearance. However, race has no scientific merit outside sociological classifications. There are no significant genetic variations within the human species to justify the division of races.

With the above definition in mind Dr. Degruy outlines the differences between white racism versus Black racism. In her view white racism adversely impacts the lives of Black people as a group, e.g. economically, by virtue of discriminatory hiring practices, limited access to healthcare and over representation in the criminal justice system and under representation in the university system. She further points out that white racism has adversely impacted African Americans through red lining and other discriminatory practices barring them from finding housing of their choice. She then contrasts white racism with Black racism by exploring the question of how can Black racism adversely affect the lives of white people as a group. The short answer is they can't! Although Blacks may have prejudices and often hatred toward white people,

Dr. Degruy emphasizes the fact that Black people lack power to adversely affect the lives of white people as a group. She mentions that black people's feelings towards whites do not preclude a white person ability to get a loan, receive fair treatment by the justice system, acquire education, etc. Therefore, the belief that people differ biologically and genetically and that one group of people are superior to another is often reinforced and supported according to the self professed superior group's ability to exert power that will negatively impact the perceived inferior group the core components of racism in this country.

Although according to Dr. Degruy's theory Blacks are not in positions of power to collectively and adversely impact the lives of white people in this country. On the other hand, whites are indisputably in position to dramatically hinder or impede the social trajectory of Black lives in today's society.

It takes fortitude and resilience to be able to withstand the endless forms of hatred, oppression, and stereo types directed at black men in this so-called "land of the free." The question is, are all of America's residents truly free? I would venture to say that certain segments of society are in economic bondage, and as a result of such bondage alternative enterprises were created in urban areas in order to achieve the "American dream" of acquiring wealth. Various ventures, although criminal, such as prostitution, drug selling, and other forms of hustling were employed as response to being locked out of opportunities to be more than a janitor or an unskilled laborer. While on a quest to acquire wealth outside of the scope of legal and traditional means, many became victims to hyper vigilant policing of urban areas which lead to subsequent arrests. Once in custody the detainee is unable to afford adequate representation, the individual is tried, convicted and shipped off to one of the many jails and prisons which serve as modern day plantations. What happened to the "innocent until proven guilty" credo? It exists but not for the poor, who happen to be majority Black and Latino, for those in that category we receive excessively high bails, and if we are on parole or probation we are not accorded the luxury of bailing out, we have to go back and forth to court in county jail yard, shackled and handcuffed, when we appear in court all psychological tactics to make us out to be the worst criminal ever thus ultimately casting us in a guilty light. For those who are in a financial position who have not been systemically criminalized and labeled which in most cases, surprisingly these individuals are white these people are deemed innocent until proven guilty.

Alternatively, the poor defendant is often coerced into taking a plea bargain in lieu of gambling with the trial process at the risk of receiving a hefty prison sentence. The prosecutors often tell the defendant's public defender (Public Pretender) that if their client loses at trial exactly how much time he would have to do depending on what the charges are of course. In most instances when the District Attorney offers a plea agreement, that usually is an indication that the case is weak but they would still like to secure a conviction. Most defendants cut their losses so to speak and take the deal. This tactic is a tool to gain psychological leverage and to make the defendant take the deal in most cases it works. The drawback is once a defendant takes a plea bargain you forfeit the right to appeal, and one stands the risk of being victimized in the future by the system's various enhancement schemes. That means if the defendant gets out and commits another crime and suffers another conviction, he or she's prior conviction will be used as a mechanism to enhance the time for the defendant's most recent conviction.

That's why there are people in the prison system today with outlandish sentences like 200 years to life, 90 years to life and in my case 37 years to life all ramifications of California's corrupt sentencing scheme.

There's a long list of things that Black men have to endure, and the unfair sentence structure in California is just one issue of many.

Some may counter by saying that we as African American's need to stop blaming the system or the "man" for our plight in life and be accountable for our choices in life. I concede to the notion that we are accountable for the choices we make in life, whether our lives are filled with hardships and struggles, or privileges and opportunities we are responsible for shaping our own destinies. I'm only submitting that racism is deeply imbedded into the fabric of this country, and to deny this reality would be naive.

I am aware that not everyone has biases toward minorities, that's a given, but I have the ability to discern, racism, prejudice and overall biased behavior. Some may refute the validity of my insight by saying my perception is off kilter with reality, and my rebuttal is, results don't lie.

Another prevailing stereotype that I personally witness quite frequently is the assumption that Blacks are intellectually inferior, or not as smart as other races. Or if a Black person happens to transcend the stereotype by exhibiting above average intellect, the consensus becomes, "you're pretty smart for a black guy" therefore, exposing the inward assumption that all Blacks are stupid. I've witnessed people who make assumptions regarding blacks to the point that their conduct indicate that Blacks are suppose to be in an inferior position and micromanaged because their conduct dictates that Blacks can't think.

Based on my observation sadly Blacks here in this prison setting have embraced the role of being inferior, and incompetent, and perpetually persisting in a role of subordination-based on the results of my observation.

Since my arrival to Soledad on July 29th, 2015 the Black population here has been nothing more than a source of chaos and confusion.

Although the Black population may not agree with my candor regarding our collective conduct, I can't be anything other than transparent in my observations of African Americans here at Soledad State Prison. For that reason, I will continue to write the truth as I see it from an unbiased position.

I embarrassingly admit, as a whole the Black residents here are in a deplorable mental state. I say that because we seem to be oblivious to the fact that we are objects of hatred frame every race here at this facility. Although residents and staff here never voice their disdain for the African American residents here, their conduct tells the true story. Case in point, when I arrived here to Soledad we were allowed to sit at any table to eat a meal within the facility cafeteria. Normally the Blacks sat on one side of the cafeteria while eating, and the whites, Hispanics and others sat on the opposite side. Why don't other races sit with Blacks. Perhaps some may think that we are dirty, ill mannered - I don't know. What I do know is that other races here at Soledad would prefer to have very minimal contact with Blacks; they don't want to use the same shower facilities, nor share the same living quarters with Blacks. The shower arrangements are segregated in each housing unit, white and Hispanics shower in their own shower area, and the Asians and Mexican Nationals shower in their own shower area, and the Blacks shower exclusively with Blacks. Recently the administration employed a feeding procedure that is commonly preferred at other prisons, and that is requiring that all inmates fill in all the tables - in other words were forced to sit with any race. I believe the procedure was implemented as a way to regain control of quasi anarchic state of Soledad. Once the procedure was enforced many inmates opted to eat from their commissary (store) surplus rather than sit at the same table with a Black inmate. The racist views went both ways, some of the Black inmates chose not to become acclimated to the new dining hall experience. I chose to eat in the cafeteria, and I noted that many inmates were repulsed by the idea of having to sit at the same table with a Black man. I noted that many would not speak during the entire feeding episode. Many would strategically circumvent the order of the line to ensure that they were not likely to sit with a Black person. Many Blacks followed the same protocol. Not all people remained taciturn during the meal, a small percentage made small talk at the table, but collectively other races were very displeased about sharing a dining room table with a Black man.

Ninety percent of the correctional officers here at Soledad are Hispanic, what that tells me based on what I've seen since I've been at this facility is that they have a propensity to show favor to other Hispanics and bias towards others - not all but some. I have seen the collective administration turn a blind eye to blatant issues that accordingly to their own policies and procedures constitute a threat to the safety and security of the facility. For example, I've w itnessed individuals alleged to be part of the prison gang Mexican Mafia walk to and from the housing unit with a group of nothing less than four people escorting him as body guards. At any other prison this conduct is not allowed, however, here at Soledad the staff is not only aware of this and other forms of blatant posturing, but staff seems to be acting in concert with this particular group. Soledad is a facility were each time the yard is open for recreation throngs of Southern Hispanics cluster around the handball court area in anticipation of their rivals - the Bulldogs - to come out to the yard and immediately get attacked.

I've been to quite a few prisons and all of the facilities I've done time at you are not allowed to participate in group exercises or call cadence or participate in any paramilitary structured workout routines. I recall when I was in the maximum security prison New Folsom no more than two could work out together, but here at Soledad paramilitary group exercising is the norm.

On any given day you will see Southern Hispanic inmates doing military exercises in groups on the yard. The administrative rank and file along with custody staff dare not utter a word against their activities.

These groups are not subtle by no means, when they congregate in numbers ranging from 15 to 200 their intent is not to pick a soccer team, or talk about the latest rehabilitative group they've attended - their sole purpose is to engage in violent riotous activity.

Yet the same officers that wont formulate a word to these particular groups are the same ones that would walk up to me while I'm visiting my wife to alert me that I'm sitting too close to her the same officers that have pulled me over in the corridor just before I walk out to the yard to tell me that I'm not allowed to wear a tank top in the corridor. Yet Soledad's officers allow Sureños, associates to the Mexican Mafia, and bona fide members of the Mexican Mafia to function with impunity.

Meanwhile African Americans continue to be the objects of hate by inmates and staff alike, and the most intense form of hatred that we have to contend with is the hate we have for each other.

African American's here at Soledad continue to be divided , and we continue to subscribe to tribalized ideologies, i.e. Crips and Bloods, North and South geographic issues, and plain ignorance coupled with jealousy.

In this microcosm of society things are predicated on position and power. Based on the prison politics that are in place each race is in a constant state of struggle to secure position and power. Everything that inmates have access to represents an opportunity to secure position and power. If an inmate has access to state soap, toilet paper, paper, paperclips, he can use the items to leverage position and power, especially if he has exclusive access to those items. Most inmates sell these and other items in order to support themselves or to supplement their income. Others secure these positions in order to be in a position to benefit their collective race or specific gang that they may be affiliated with. For instance, the housing clerk is one of the most sought after and coveted positions an inmate can occupy while in prison. The reason being, inmates in this position are given a large measure of power by virtue of the correctional officer that employ them. In most cases they are given carte blanche to process bed moves, pass out various legal forms - as needed by inmates - the clerk also distributes cleaning supplies, as well as soap and toilet paper. As a whole the inmate clerk has access to a copious amount of resources and often a well established rapport with officers. These inmates are often shielded from routine cell searches, and on many occasions afforded the luxury of acquiring the contraband frequently taken out of inmate's cell during routine cell searches. This position is highly sought after by all races with the exclusion of Blacks. There are Blacks in these positions but the percentage of African Americans in these positions is extremely low. This prestigious position which is frequently filled by those who are anti - Black can serve as a vehicle to systemically oppress certain inmates. Quite frankly, these inmate housing clerks have the power to make your time in prison uncomfortable to a certain degree.

I've witnessed here at Soledad men remain in their assigned cells without ever receiving a cell - mate for years, simply because they have a rapport with the housing clerk. On the flip side, I've witnessed inmates who were only without a cell - mate for maybe a couple of weeks and as soon as a new inmate arrives they are the first ones to get a cell - mate. The housing clerk literally suggests to the officers that the new inmate should be placed in a particular cell. Here at Soledad a small dose of freedom can be achieved if one is allowed to remain in his assigned cell without the likes of having a cell - mate who in most cases is not compatible with his cell - mate. Most of the time inmates assigned to housing clerk positions are unreasonable and arrogant. These inmates are often used by officers as their "eyes and ears." They often supply officers with information about other inmates to ensure the solidification of their clerk position.

Not only are Black men throughout California's prison complex dealing with vindictive and oppressive inmates in positions of power, we also contend with officers who are in cahoots with certain inmates to intentionally keep even prisoners in an inferior position even while incarcerated.

In my experience of incarceration, inmates in these prestigious positions are some of the most deceptive and scandalous people I've ever encountered most of these inmates are dope fiends, gang members who are deeply entrenched in prison politics.

To illustrate: Imagine going to a fast food restaurant and ordering food. When you pick up your order it's not what you ordered. Discontent With the service you request to speak with the manager, when he motions to speak with you its obvious that he's under the influence of a controlled substance - perhaps heroin. To make matters worse he has racist views toward African American's, so your grievance falls on deaf ears. Similarly, that's what it's like dealing with a lot of these arrogant morally devoid, and drug addicted inmates here in Soledad. I've been dealing with one in particular who in my view is a racist and intoxicated with the power the officers have allowed him to have. In fact based on his conduct he thinks he is an officer.

The Black population here collectively doesn't possess any power to make things happen, and due to the racial prison politics other races make sure systematically they are blocked from certain key positions. Even with their attempts to block their paths to gain access to coveted prison resources and other forms of privilege, some manage to muscle their way into positions.

Some within the ranks of the African American community have the drive and determination and aren't deterred by the obvious racial impediments that permeate most California prison environments.

On the other hand, those of us that don't have drive to get past the mental restrictions that we place on ourselves are in a deplorable situation. Not only are a large number of African American men here at Soledad in a disparaging condition, it appears, based on results, that they want to remain in a state mediocrity.

There are guys here who have been locked up for over three decades and have yet to obtain a high school diploma, and sadly they have no intentions of completing a basic high school education.

We as African American's have high rates of hyper tension and diabetes because we have and unquenchable addiction to sugar and salt and a phobia for eating healthy. Here at Soledad we as African American will purchase junk food for the facility commissary on a monthly basis, at the expense of our family and friends and consume copious amounts of junk until we become bloated and overweight. We will consume every product known to man, but we won't figure out ways to produce anything.

Aside from being hated from all angles by other races, African Americans are rivals of each other. We cannot get along to achieve a common cause, the bottom line is we don't like each other, and constantly put each other down rather than encourage one another.

On any given day I can walk out of my cell and walk past a group of Blacks and hear them either gossiping about another African American in an attempt to spread false and malicious rumors about another person. Or speak to someone and as soon as he walks away the back biting begins.

We place barriers between ourselves based on geographic factors, or gang affiliations, which only serves to stifle our forward progression. We are so divided and self centered that we won't take time to get to know one another, unless we there's a hidden agenda-something we can benefit from, it seems that everything is predicated on usury. People often befriend others here in this prison environment for the exclusive purpose of using you. We as Black men are in a bad space here at Soledad, and it seems to be getting worse.

We are so desensitized when it comes to caring for one another, we have no real connection to each other, which only speaks to lack of love for self. Love for self is not in the context of selfishness; it simply acknowledging our individual value, it's not ignorance, it's developing healthy self-esteem and understanding who we are as well as what we are capable of.

Until we come to the realization that we are valuable we will never make any headway in America.

We continue to perpetuate the validity of stereotypes by walking around in public wearing "Du rags" on our heads, being loud and obnoxious, fathering illegitimate children, and shunning our responsibility as fathers. Until we step up and be examples to our children we will only teach them how to expedite their death by participating in unsavory activity such as crime, gangs, sexual promiscuity and the like. We can't blame them for following the model that we set for them-we have to be better role models for our youth. It's time to break the cycle of poverty, violence, drug addiction, and self hate.

Our prisons are filled with African American and Latino men and women who were misguided, men and women who were socialized to hate other races, men and women who learned how to be violent due in part to flawed thinking coupled with mimicking what they saw others do. These men and women thought violence was the only way to gain respect in an urban jungle. That line of reasoning is diseased, I humbly submit the way to earn respect is to respect yourself and others and position yourself in the best light possible and others will in turn respect you.

Otherwise if the cycle is not broken and if we don't change our trajectory in life we will continue to be viewed as an inferior people who are intractable and always in the clutches of those who subscribe to the notion that we can't think, and our only role is a subordinate position.

License to Kill

As a kid I witnessed my father hit my mother. After witnessing such a traumatic experience at the tender age of seven, I was left emotionally damaged and psychologically scared. As a by - product of that episode I developed a resentment toward authority figures. This resentment was the birth of my intense hatred for my father at the time. Growing up I subconsciously equated male authority with my unresolved hatred aimed at my father.

1 had no clue back in 1977, at seven years old that my anger toward my father would be displaced and directed at everyone but my father later in my life.

When I was thirteen years old in 1983 I was ordered by the courts to spend time in a boy's home for robbing a kid my age at knife point for his bike. I was sent from juvenile hall to a home named Hathaway Home For Children, located in Highland Park, California. It was during this juncture of my young life that my unresolved hatred would come to surface in a displaced manner.

While at Hathaway my adjustment to the rules wasn't met with any resistance until one Thursday night during the month of January, 1983.

Don Pestana, was a staff member at Hathaway. Don was a Caucasian man, with a slim build, and reddish shoulder length hair, and wire rimmed glasses. He looked like a reformed hippie who was trying to straighten out his life. Don was maybe in his late twenties at the time.

On this particular night I happened to be walking in the hallway of the house I was assigned to reside in - along with five other young boys. On this defining night Don and another staff were tasked with supervising the young boys in the cottage - as the house was referred to.

Our behavior was punished or rewarded by on what amounted to an individual merit ladder, and at the end of the week the boys who exhibited positive behavior and it was visibly reflected on ones chart, that individual would be afforded the opportunity to go on a "Home pass" for the weekend. I personally lived for the end of the week because that meant I could potentially go home for the weekend to spend time with my mother and visit neighborhood friends.

As I motioned through the hallway Don was writing on our charts which were on a bulletin board in the hallway. As I walked by I glanced intently at the remarks Don was making on my chart. I can't remember what those remarks said, but I do know they would prevent me from going home for the weekend. I became very agitated by Don's action and I verbally expressed my displeasure by hurling a few choice expletives at him. He then demanded that I go to my room. I then informed him in no uncertain terms that I wasn't going anywhere. In a rage of anger I briskly walked to the utility closet and grabbed a broom while Don continued to write negative comments and seeming unscathed by my barrage of verbal assaults. The broom I retrieved had plastic bristles, and a plastic casing just above the bristles.

I rushed back to Don with broom in hand, and in a blind rage I struck Don in the eye; I immediately observed the crack in Don's glasses accompanied by the visible thick concentration of blood surrounding the surface of Don's eye. Don yelled for assistance and commenced to tackle me to the ground, more staff arrived and I was restrained. I was allowed to go back to my room after the particulars of the incident were obtained. The next morning 1 woke up to the presence of a Burbank Police Officer and the head of Hathaway.

My next conflict with an authority figure took place while I was in Los Padrinos Juvenile Hall located in Downey, California. I was there on this particular occasion for a parole violation. The year was 1985 and I hadn't been released from the California Youth Authority not even two months before 1 was back in custody for a dirty cocaine test and failing to attend high school.

I was somewhat hardened at 15 after having survived the combative climate of Fred C. Nelles (California Youth Authority), so in my mind and in my actions 1 carried myself as if I was in the big leagues in terms of the juvenile justice system, and back then the wards of Los Padrinos who never went to Y.A. looked at those who have been, as someone who has been to gladiator school. It was a status symbol of sorts. I was housed in one Los Padrinos many units called "R - S." All of the housing units were named after letters of the alphabet, e.g. A - B, C - D. E - F, G - H, L - M, T - U, R - S, and X - Y.

On this particular afternoon the entire unit was eating lunch in the area known as the "day room." Everyone was instructed by the unit staff to remain "on quiet" as we ate our lunch. The unit counselor made this announcement, as we stood over our trays awaiting the opportunity to eat. He then instructed everyone to bow their head and have a moment of silence to pray, he then instructed us to be seated. Everything was very regimented.

I was defiant at the time and I quickly disregarded the order to remain taciturn. I initiated a brief conversation with the gentleman directly in front of the table I was sitting at. I proceeded to converse while eating an apple when suddenly the staff walks in from his office and approached me from behind and slapped the apple out of my mouth in a motion likened to a clap. He then yells at me in a very aggressive tone, "didn't I tell you it was on quiet? Take it to your room!" Angry, and humiliated in front of everyone, I reluctantly and slowly walked down the hallway to my room without being able to finish my lunch.

About two minutes after the event I was in my room and the counselor came into my room in an attempt to talk to me about the issue of insubordination. Steaming with anger I immediately assaulted the counselor as he furiously yelled for help. Several staff assisted him; I was subsequently choked, restrained and taken to the "box"

(Isolation).

With each negative experience I encountered with those in position of authority my level of suspicion and distrust increased.

To put things in context regarding my views of authority as I grew up I must answer the question: How did I view law enforcement officials?

As I mentioned at the outset, I witnessed domestic abuse as a child, and in recall an issue in 1975 when my family and I lived in Lynwood, California on a street named Woodlawn, my father was abusing my mother. I remember hearing the heated argument, and the angry expressions on my father's face spurred on by intoxicating amounts of Crown Royal Whiskey. I recall my mother running out the door of our humble abode in an attempt to escape the imminent physical abuse of my father. She managed to go to the neighbor's house and call the police. I remember her returning accompanied by the Lynwood police and they briefly spoke to my father, and then asked my mom if she had anywhere that her and her kids could go for the night. Nothing was done to my father although he was the aggressor, and we ultimately had to leave the house for the night. That incident helped shape a negative view of the police in my mind.

I viewed them as untrustworthy. In fact, many of my counterparts share similar sentiments.

I spoke with a young man on the yard by the name of Tiny Bosco from a gang called Carver Park Crips, located in Compton, California. When asked what his views of the police were growing up he stated that as a kid he recalled the police coming to his elementary school issuing baseball cards to the students, so at such a young age he thought that the police were friendly. He went on to express to me that as he grew onto his teenage years, the same officers who were handing out baseball cards when he was in elementary became the officers who would harass him for what he viewed as no reason. He stated that they would often come through his neighborhood and line all of his homies up and document each one for what would tater prove to be a gang identification file. He stated that having experienced such treatment his view of the police became one of hatred and distrust. Other people that I've talked to articulated to me that their hatred and distrust for law enforcement was cemented in their minds and hearts at very young ages. They were taught by their parents not to trust the police, and if you had an issue that needed to be taken care of or if someone did something to you - never snitch.

With this small glimpse into the psychology of why urban residents - many of them at least - hate law enforcement.

In contrast, when trying to understand the psychology of police behavior we must first address the mindset of the current culture of some officers who are indiscriminately killing, in most cases, unarmed Black men.

I can honestly say that looking back at the negative encounter I've had with Police Officers, the things I did during that time period would definitely have caused me to be shot and killed by the police according to today's hypersensitive police culture.

In 1990 I had a run in with officers of the Pomona Police Department which started as a foot chase and ended with my brother and I fighting the officers which ultimately resulted in me receiving a broken hand due to being hit with the "Billy club" and the subsequent arrest of my brother and I. In today's times, that incident would have, more likely than not resulted in the death of my brother and I.

Today police agencies across the United States are super intolerant, and subconsciously fearful of Black males. As a direct result Black males are being killed at the hand of police.

August 9, 2014 Michael Brown was shot to death by a white officer in Ferguson Missouri, it awakened a movement that began with the previous killing of another Black teenager, Trayvon Martin who was shot in 2012 by neighborhood watch volunteer George

Zimmerman.

Also in 2014, Donte Hamilton 31 was fatally shot 14 times by police in a Milwaukee park. The officer was responding to a call from employees at a nearby Starbucks alleging that Hamilton, who had been diagnosed with paranoid schizophrenia, was disturbing the peace. The officers who arrived first determined that Hamilton wasn't doing anything illegal. Officer Christopher Manney showed up later and after trying to pat Hamilton down engaged in a struggle with him that led to the shooting. Manney was not charged.

On July 17, 2014 in New York, Eric Gamer, 43 was killed after he was put in an illegal chokehold for 15 seconds by a white officer - allegedly for selling loose cigarettes. Gamer said. "I can't breathe" 11 times as he was held down by several on a sidewalk. The officer who put Garner in a chokehold, Daniel Pantaleo, was not charged.

August 5, 2014 in Dayton Ohio, John Crawford, 22 was shot and killed by a police officer at a Wal-Mart. There did not seem to be a confrontation with the police and Crawford was unarmed - he had been holding a BB gun. The officers involved in the shooting, Sean Williams and David Darkow, were not charged.

These are just a few examples of the many African American males who were unarmed and yet the end result was death at the hands of law enforcement officers. Police killed 1,147 people in 2017. Black people were 25% of those killed despite being only 13% of the population.

Studies have found that Black people are shot by police at disproportionate rates, and unarmed victims are more likely to be Black according to a 2018 Harvard study, black men age 15 to 34 are nine to 16 times more likely to be killed by police than other people. Policies that mandate training and body cameras have not stopped the brutality. They've only reinforced what they already believe: too many law enforcement officers have no respect for the lives in Black communities they police.

Since 2005, 98 police officers have been arrested, and only 35 convicted to date, according to the Police Integrity Research Group at Bowling Green State University.

These are just a few examples of the many African American males who were unarmed and yet the end result was death at the hands of law enforcement officers. Police killed 1,147 people in 2017. Black people were 25% of those killed despite being only 13% of the population.

Studies have found that Black people are shot by police at disproportionate rates, and unarmed victims are more likely to be Black according to a 2018 Harvard study, Black men age 15 to 34 are nine to 16 times more likely to be killed by police than other people. Policies that mandate training and body cameras have not stopped the brutality. They've only reinforced what they already believe: too many law enforcement officers have no respect for the lives in Black communities they police.

Since 2005, 98 police officers have been arrested, and only 35 convicted to date, according to the Police Integrity Research Group at Bowling Green State University.

Some theorize that killing of unarmed Black men at the hands of the police is essentially an undeclared campaign aimed at traumatizing the very conscience of mind, sending a clear message that police have gone from protecting and serving, to killing and lying. Their favorite excuse is, "I thought he had a weapon." That simple one line phrase represents their justification to end human life by uttering the word, "I feared for my life." This is nothing more than conjecture and the legal equivalent to having a license to kill.

Black men in this country are feared, labeled as criminals who are prone to violence. Despite the training officers receive if an officer views Black men through such biased lenses the outcome will always end with another Black man shot and killed simply for being born Black.

What needs to be done to end these heart wrenching crimes perpetrated by the police under the color of authority? I will admit it won't be an easy fix, and I also know that the police have a very dangerous job to perform, and by no means does that give them the right to whimsically and arbitrarily kill unarmed Black men.

I think a large reason why police officers overreact when dealing with Black men is deeply rooted in fear. This fear stems from how they've been socialized to perceive Black men especially larger and darker men - they are stereotyped as being extremely aggressive and violent.

We are constantly viewed with a suspicious eye. And we are often assumed to have committed a crime or in the process of committing an illegal act. When officers approach all Black men with this distorted line of reasoning it becomes a self fulfilling prophecy - "I believe he is dangerous and threatening.' 'Therefore,' 'I must eliminate the threat.' 'Then afterward, 'I'll lie and say; I thought he had a weapon,' or 'I feared for my life so I discharged X amount of rounds from my service weapon."

This has to stop! Black men have to feel safe as anyone else, yet this is not the case when confronted by police. A mere traffic violation turns into your family preparing your funeral arrangements.

As long as we as Black men are viewed in an unfavorable light, I only foresee things getting worse.

Solutions

Now that we know some of the issues that plague our society, the question becomes what is the solution. Attempts to correct flawed, greedy, and violent society that we live in would definitely be met with resistance. Generations upon generations of hate have been etched into the minds and hearts of this racist and capitalistic society.

The simple formula for the present woes that exist in today's modem and highly technical world we live in is love. If we come to the realization that we are all human beings, who are striving for equality. We all want the highest quality of life possible, unfortunately quality of life is a luxury accorded to a privileged few.

The simple formula for the present woes that exist in today's modern and highly technical world we live in is love. If we come to the realization that we are all human beings, who are striving for equality. We all want the highest quality of life possible, unfortunately quality of life is a luxury accorded to a privileged few.

We as a society must express love for all of humanity through our deeds and actions. When we as a society learn to cultivate love we will also bear the fruits of compassion, empathy, and humility.

We need compassion in order to help someone who is in dire straits. We need compassion to understand that we all are imperfect human beings and subject to err. We need compassion to forgive someone who may have wronged us. We need to place more value on human lives than we do our dogs and cats.

We need to empathize with the plight of others. We need to follow the "Golden Rule" and treat others the way would want to be treated, and in our everyday dealings with people we need to ask ourselves simple questions, "How would I feel if someone mistreated me?" "How would I feel if someone hurt me the way I've hurt others in the past?" Once we meditate on feeling another person's pain and suffering, we will be more apt to treat all people with dignity and respect regardless of their race, regardless of their economic situation, and regardless of their religion. At the end of the day, people are people. It's only when greed, jealousy, and fear enter the equation do we develop a need to feel superior to others and to oppress others to insure they don't acquire certain positions of power. The fear of losing power and control historically has only resulted in wars and loss of life. The country is founded on greed and violence, and these evil elements are still in existence today. Until we apply the fundamental qualities of love there will always be the powerful and the oppressed.

Humility is the absence of pride and arrogance, humility is the ability to view others as superior to you, and to put their needs ahead of your own. Basically humility is being selfless, instead of selfish. The world needs more selflessness instead of selfishness and arrogance. We live in a society where people only care about their selfish needs and desires. In fact, people are lovers of themselves, self assuming haughty, unthankful, and disloyal. The common thread of all these characteristics is selfishness. Until we as a society step back and get out of our selfish way of thinking and behaving there will always be those who will be victims of the tangled web of deceit called Urban Genocide.

"Woe to those who enact harmful regulations, who constantly draft oppressive decrees, to deny the legal claim of the poor, to deprive the lowly among my people of justice, making widows their spoils and fatherless children their plunder! What will you do on the day of reckoning, when destruction comes from afar? To whom will you flee for assistance, and where will you leave your wealth? Nothing remains except to crouch among the prisoners...".

ISAIAH 10; 1-4

Humility is the absence of pride and arrogance, humility is the ability to view others as superior to you, and to put their needs ahead of your own. Basically humility is being selfless, instead of selfish. The world needs more selflessness instead of selfishness and arrogance. We live in a society where people only care about their selfish needs and desires. In fact, people are lovers of themselves, self assuming haughty, unthankful, and disloyal. The common thread of all these characteristics is selfishness. Until we as a society step back and get out of our selfish way of thinking and behaving there will always be those who will be victims of the tangled web of deceit called Urban Genocide.

94

The Face Behind the Mask

During slavery days black's were viewed as subhuman, lazy, ignorant and hypersexual beings. Yet their extraordinary physical strength, endurance, and stamina was exploited for the capital gains of the slave owners.

Slaves were prohibited from learning how to read or write. This begs the question as to why would someone be adamant about preventing someone to improve and develop mentally. The answer is simple, if slaves learned how to read they would have learned how to think critically, and perhaps that would come to the realization that they were being exploited. So being able to think during slavery days was frowned upon - the slave owners did the thinking for slaves, and slaves were punished for trying to think independently apart from being told how to think.

The bottom line is, once we as an oppressed people, whether black, white, green or purple, figure out how to think independent of being taught what to think, at that point we become a threat to the status quo. Now we pose a threat to people in positions of power because we could figure out a way to secure position, there by securing power.

The slave owners perhaps thought that if slaves were educated they could see the overall scheme and potentially overthrow them from their reign of terror.

The underlying reason for Blacks being prohibited from learning how to read is fear. Fear that somehow these once viewed as lazy, ignorant Negroes may suddenly become enlightened and capable of overthrowing the evil and oppressive institution of slavery. Today that subconscious fear of African American's is still in existence. Why? For as long as I can remember, African American's have been inappropriately labeled and stereotyped as a means to justify the lack of familiarity of Black culture. It's been said that "man fears the unknown." Therefore, if one is not acquainted with a culture of people it's human nature to fear it. It's not human nature however; to create our own narrative about people we are afraid to become familiar with. Most of the negative narrative associated with African American's is conjecture at best.

Until we as a society get away from the negative conjecture, theories, and speculation as to who African American's are inherently, we will continue to hear about police killing unarmed Black men, we will continue to see people of other nationalities commit crimes and use Blacks as scapegoats.

In order to dispels these false notions that Blacks are lazy, loud, and ignorant we must embrace our society's commonalities instead of always highlighting our differences.

We need to stop feeding our minds with the notion that one race is superior to another and realize we are all part of the big melting pot called the human race, we were all created the exact same way, with the qualities of God ingrained in us - Love.

Until we erase arrogance and superiority from our minds and hearts and cultivate humility, this world will continue to be a hate filled and violent place.

On the flip side we as African American's must stop believing the negative narratives and learn how to think independently and creatively, as opposed to being taught how we should think. I'm addressing this issue because if someone continues to tell you that you are lazy, you are dumb, you are a criminal, eventually you will internalize it, and your beliefs about yourself will become manifest in your conduct. We have to transcend the negative stereotypes and believe that we are the complete opposite of those false narratives associated with us as African Americans.

We have - as the results indicate - internalized a lot of the false labels that have been drilled into our psyche since birth. As a result when we interact with other people of color, since we have subscribed to the notion that we are worthless, we project those feelings towards others that look like us. This self hatred has been the foundation for many Black on Black crimes committed in this country.

It's been my experience that the crabs in the barrel analogy is true when it comes to trying to progress in the urban areas we learned from the example of Nipsey Hussle's untimely demise. Although he was a very successful rap artist who was embraced and loved by the community he hailed from, there's always one jealous person who can't stand to see the next man succeed. There was more to the story surrounding his death, but when we peel the layers back the root cause was jealousy - in my view.

There's so many issues - social ills that may or may not be remedied in my life time, but if we individually do our part to effect social change, I believe we can change the dynamics of our society.

Urban genocide is real, and until we become aware of the strategic traps - if you will - that are placed in our path we will continue to kill each other at high rates, we will continue to be systemically lockout of various economic opportunities, we will continue to be alcoholics and drug addicts, and we will continue to consume large amounts of unhealthy food. We must break the cycle of urban genocide.

98

Epilogue

During my 17 years of incarceration I've exerted myself vigorously to change the mind and heart of the person I am within, it's not about projecting an outward appearance in an attempt to deceive - true change begins on the inside and then manifests itself through conduct. The parable in the book of Matthew tells us that, ".. .a good tree cannot bear worthless fruit, not can a rotten tree produce fine fruit." In essence the point of that illustration is to high light that you can identify a man whether good or bad by his conduct. When we ponder the issues taking place in the world we could only conclude that the fruit of the world's tree is completely rotten. Violence is deeply rooted in the fabric of this country; high standards of morality seem to be an ever fading virtue, only to be replaced with what society terms "alternative lifestyles," a semantical way of describing debauchery.

The sanctity of marriage is being breached and replaced with a union contrary to nature, and our very children are being taught in schools that this behavior is simply another facet of love.

Condom dispensers are now placed in men's prison facilities which deafeningly points not only to the desensitizing of our society but also the "anything goes'' approach taken by the current climate of today's culture.

The spike in police shootings, mass incarceration, and drug use in epidemic proportions only highlights the United States is a country in desperate need of repair.

We live in a world where hate and racism is as common as the air we breathe, a place where people of color are treated with spite and distain, a place where disproportionate numbers of Blacks and Latino's overwhelm the nation's prisons and jails, a place where one out of four

Black males are on parole or probation, a place where conditions are created to entrap us, to foster our failure, and stifle our economic mobility.

All anyone wants is equality. Race doesn't matter - at least it shouldn't matter. We all want the same opportunities to take part in free enterprise known as capitalism without inordinate and often insurmountable obstacles placed before the undesirable segments of people confined to urban areas of this diabolical and sadistic society we live in.

My purpose for exploring these sensitive and controversial topics is not *take a pro black stance and anti white*; that's not my agenda. I don't have a racist bone in my body. My purpose is to shed light on reality. The reality of it is, we live in a racist country, and there are people who have historically been objects of hate, systemically treated unfairly.

It's not about shifting blame; it's about being aware of the social ills in existence and taking steps toward tearing down those obstacles and barriers that have been strategically placed before us. Once we raise awareness levels then we reduce the likelihood of being victims of various forms of exploitation, thereby escaping the clutches of Urban Genocide.

1 grew up being part of the problem as it relates to urban genocide. I witnessed a lot of dysfunction domestically and socially, and I grew to believe that these issues were just the way life was. I didn't know any better. As an adult I've learned through trial and error it was my choices that landed me in and out of incarceration since age twelve. Granted the conditions were in place for me to fail, however, I had the choice to make my conditions better. I take full responsibility for the choices I've made in life. Today I have channeled those negative experiences into something positive and productive. If I can help someone by virtue of sharing my negative experiences and views and insights, then I've achieved my goal of becoming a giver. Today I want to give something back to the world - as bad as things in it may

be - I now consider myself as a giver instead of a taker. The majority of my life was spent being in self centered mode. I didn't have much regard of the feelings of others, namely those who loved me, if I did I wouldn't have made the choices that took me away from those who truly cared for me and landed me in the pit of confinement.

Today after years and years of painstaking efforts to renew my mind, I can confidently say I'm no longer the selfish man I was 17 years ago. Today I genuinely care about the welfare of other's without any hidden agendas - pure concern.

The years I've spent incarcerated have given me ample time to look within myself in order to understand my many character defects. In order to change I had to be aware of what to change. I had to understand what made me who I am, I had to understand my emotions, my frustrations, my anger, my resentment, and my motive for change itself.

My motivation for change was simple - what I was doing wasn't working for me. The gang life for me only offered a false sense of loyalty, and a distorted view of the true definition of friends. I learned through experience that the ones I viewed as friends in the gang culture were actually enemies masquerading as friends; they were never friends from the start. They were just a bunch of guys who shared the same dysfunctional plight - nothing more. Through all the negative experiences I was able to gain a clear perspective on how the world works and with every choice comes a consequence.

I'm now in a unique position to shed light on social issues as I see them from my point of view. Some may not agree with my line of reasoning and that's okay, we all have the right to our opinions. However, it is my wish that my reader will be able to identify with some, it not all of the issues I've outlined. I hope the readers will take away a positive gem that will have practical value and hopefully broaden your perspective of the hidden evils that take place in this country.

As we move forward on this brief journey of life I hope that we can all put the past behind us and forgive one another in order to rid ourselves of the toxic poison called hate.

If we want to make a positive change in the world we need to start with positive examples. I certainly hope that I was able to provide you with a glimpse of the problem, as well as the simple solution which is the desperate need of love.

Today I'm an advocate for positive change; my mission in life is to be of service to others, and to change minds and hearts one book at a time.

About the Author

Charles Carpenter has managed to transcend the physical parameters of imprisonment to become a riveting and impactful empirical story teller. He cleverly weaves real life experiences into narratives with practical applications designed to change minds and hearts, one book at a time.